Dog - Perro

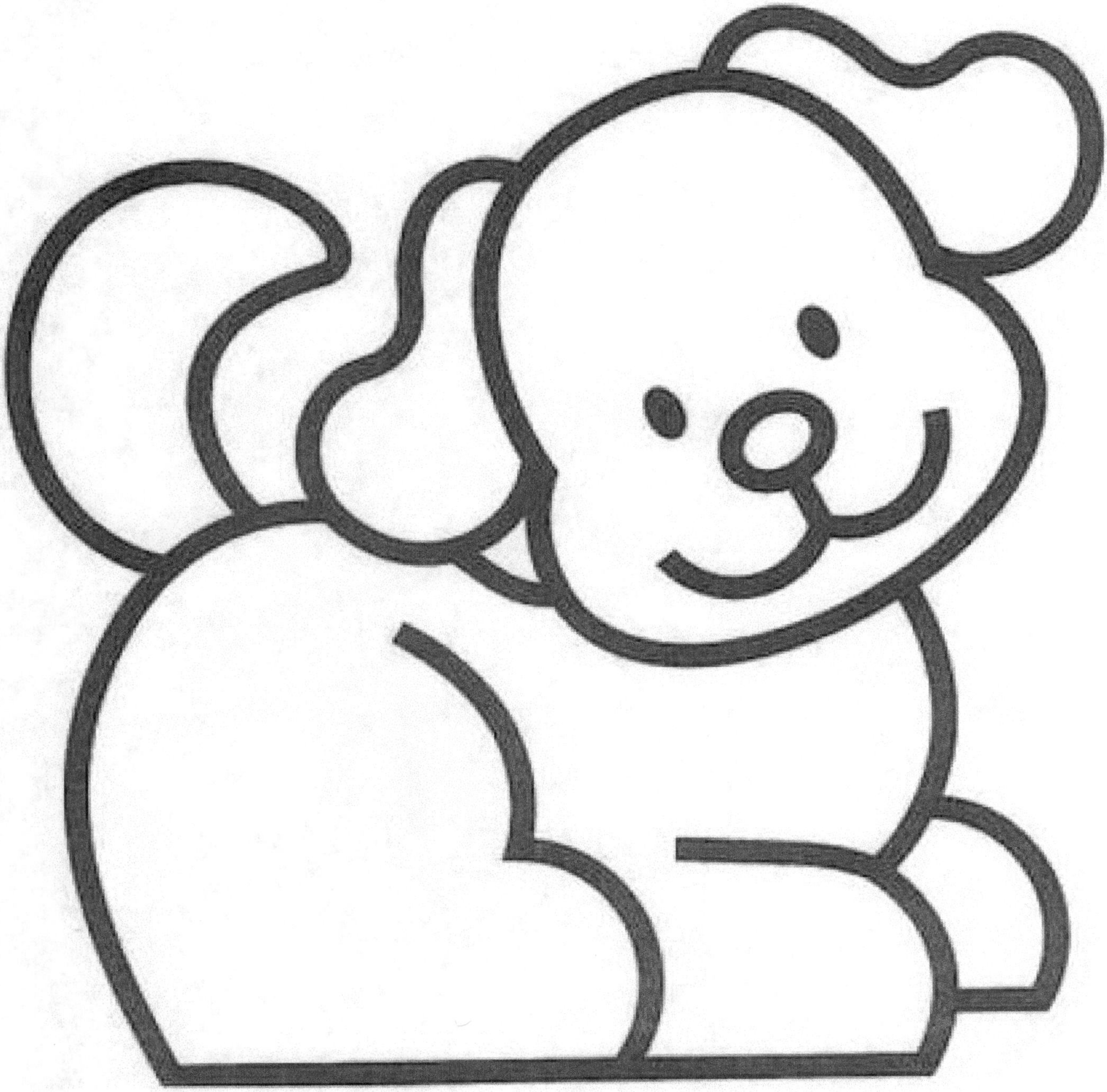

Cat - Gato

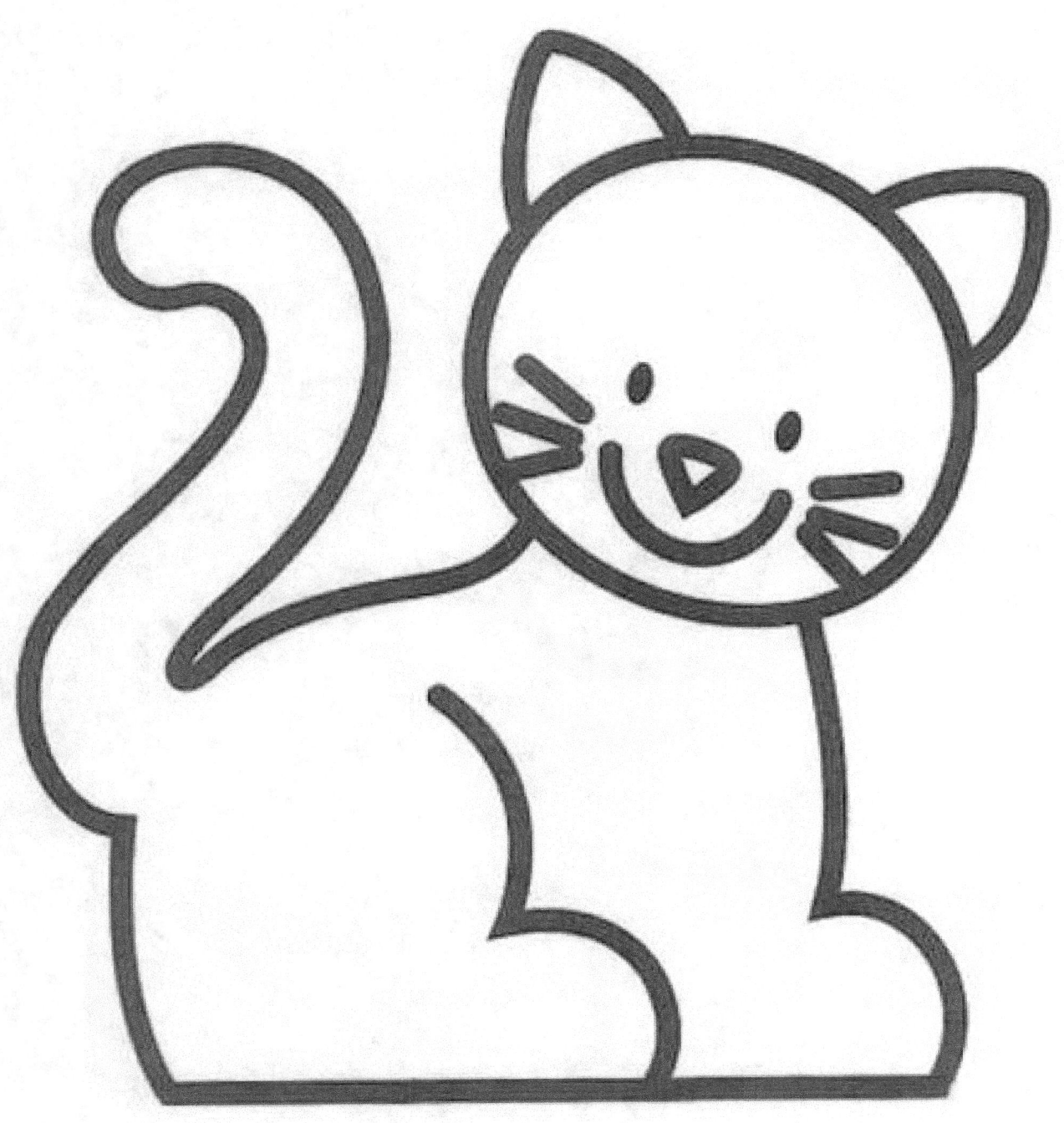

Duck - Pato

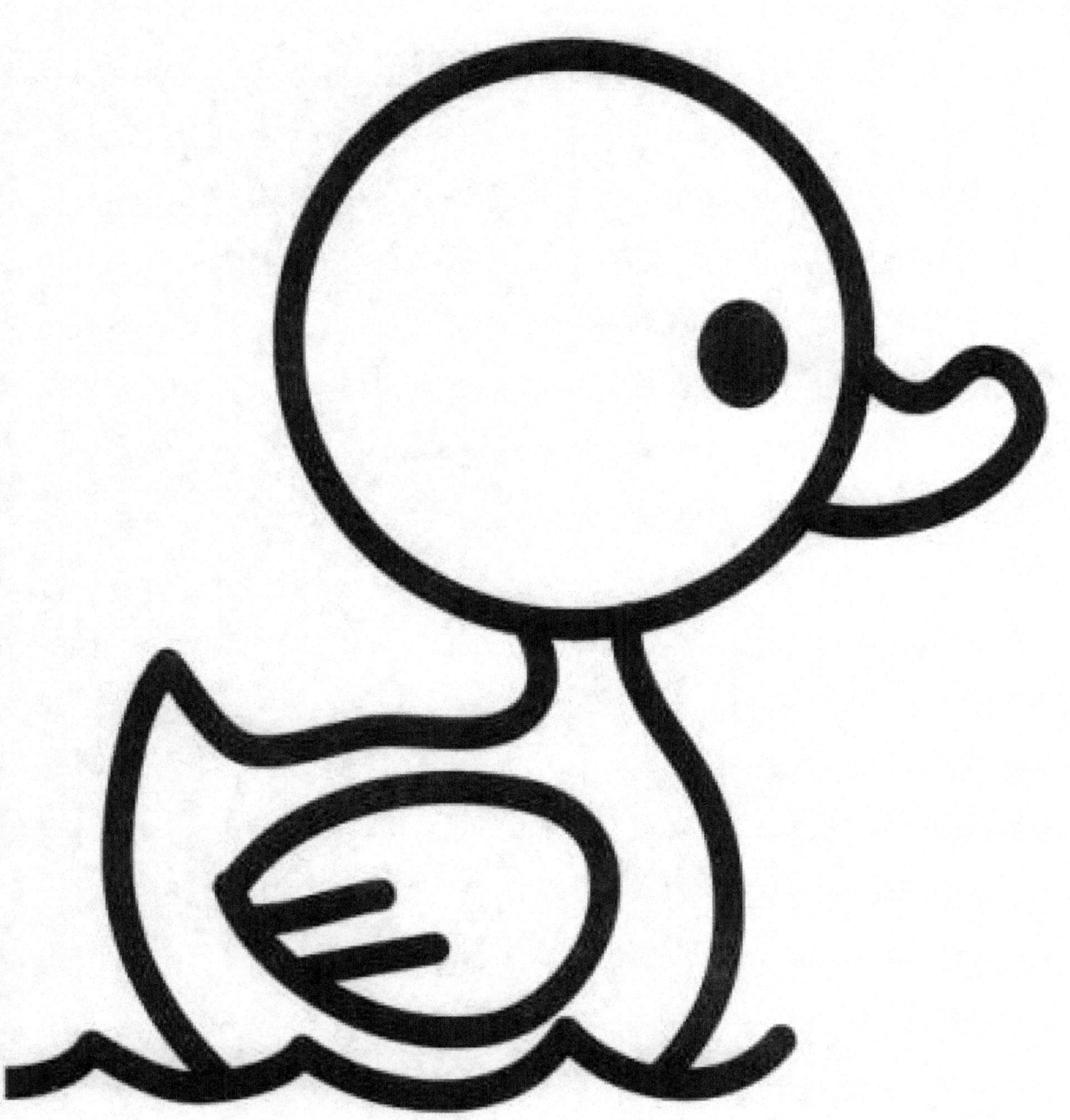

Rooster - Gallo

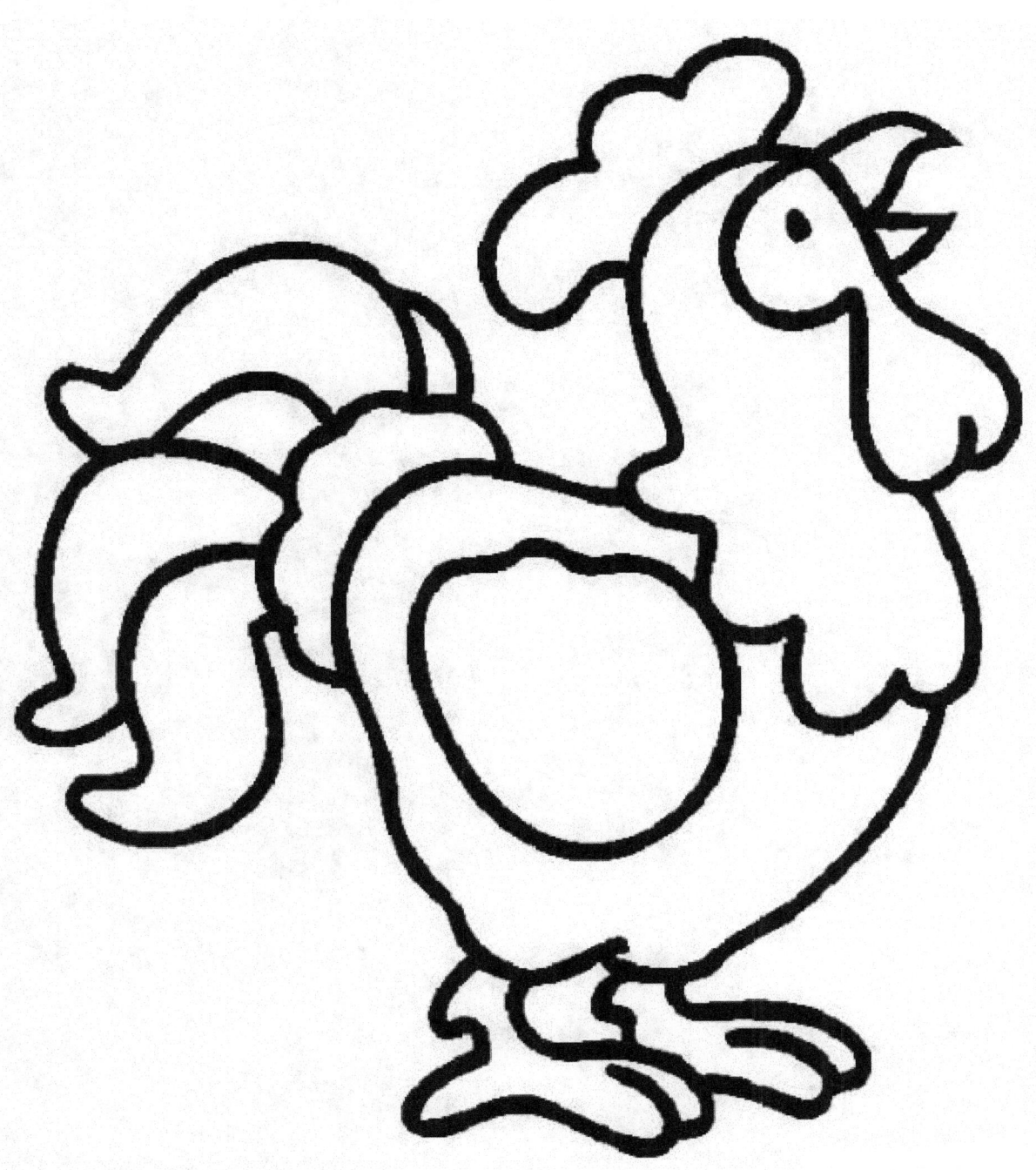

Hen - Gallina

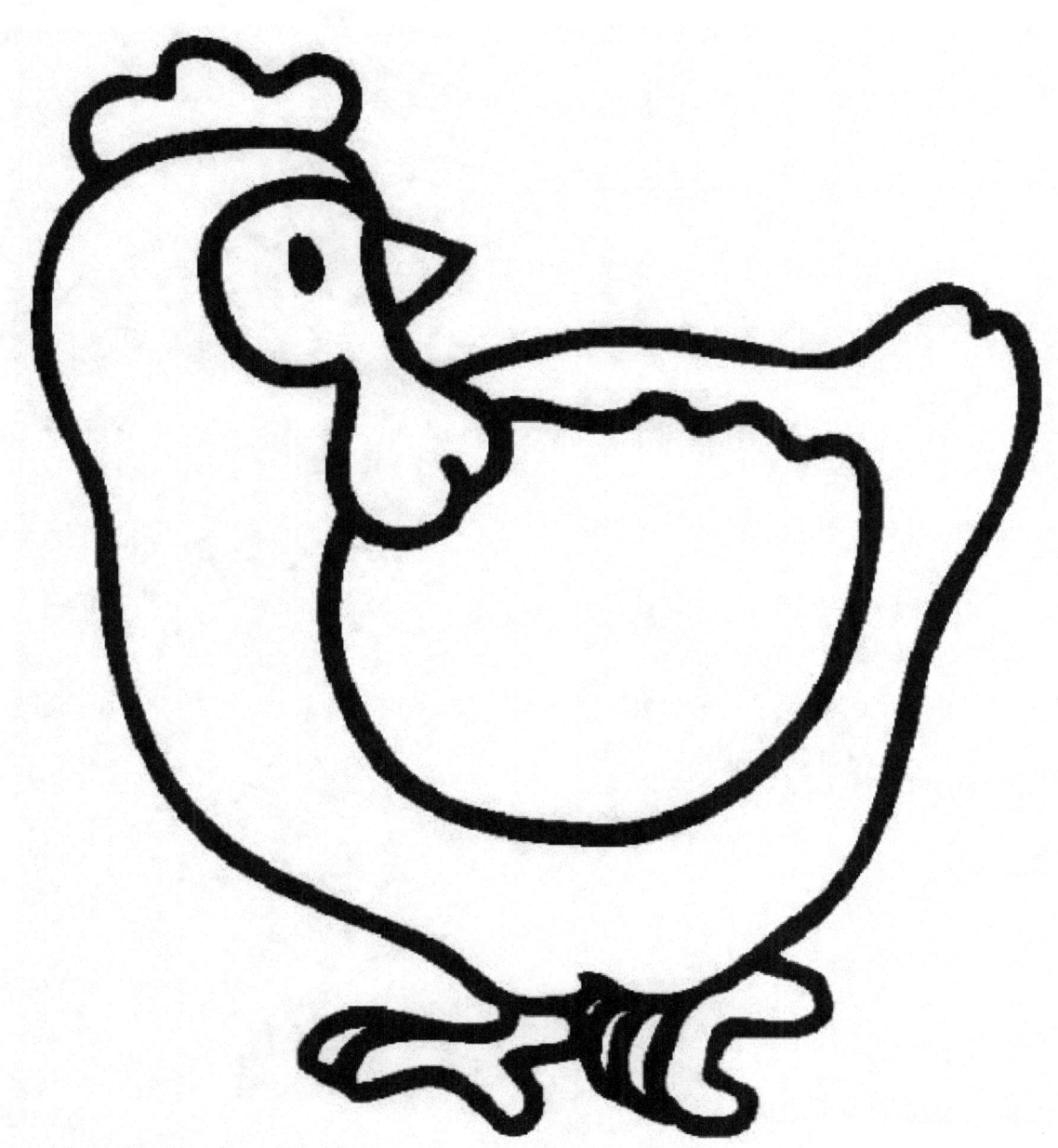

Pig – Puerco

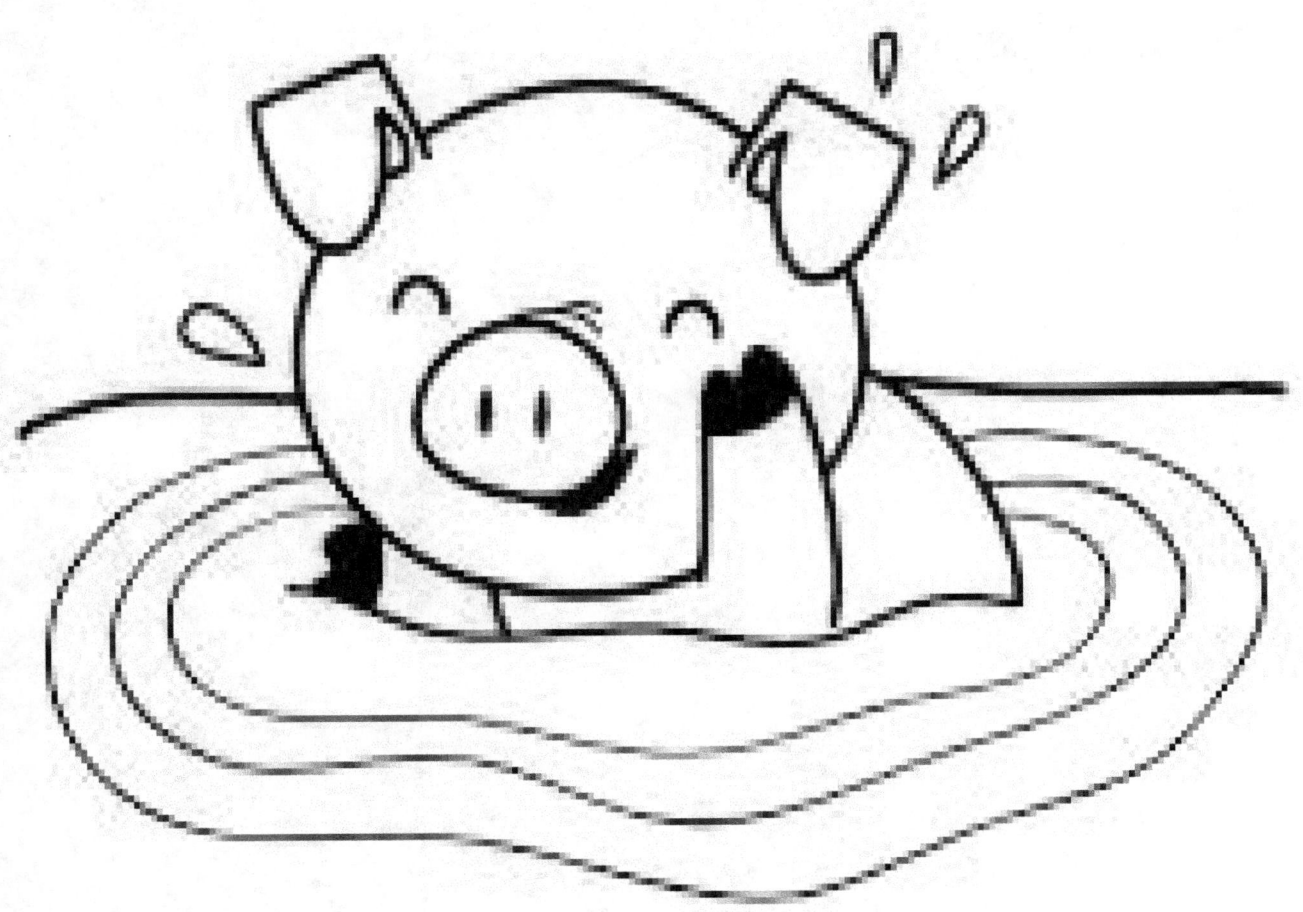

Cow - Vaca

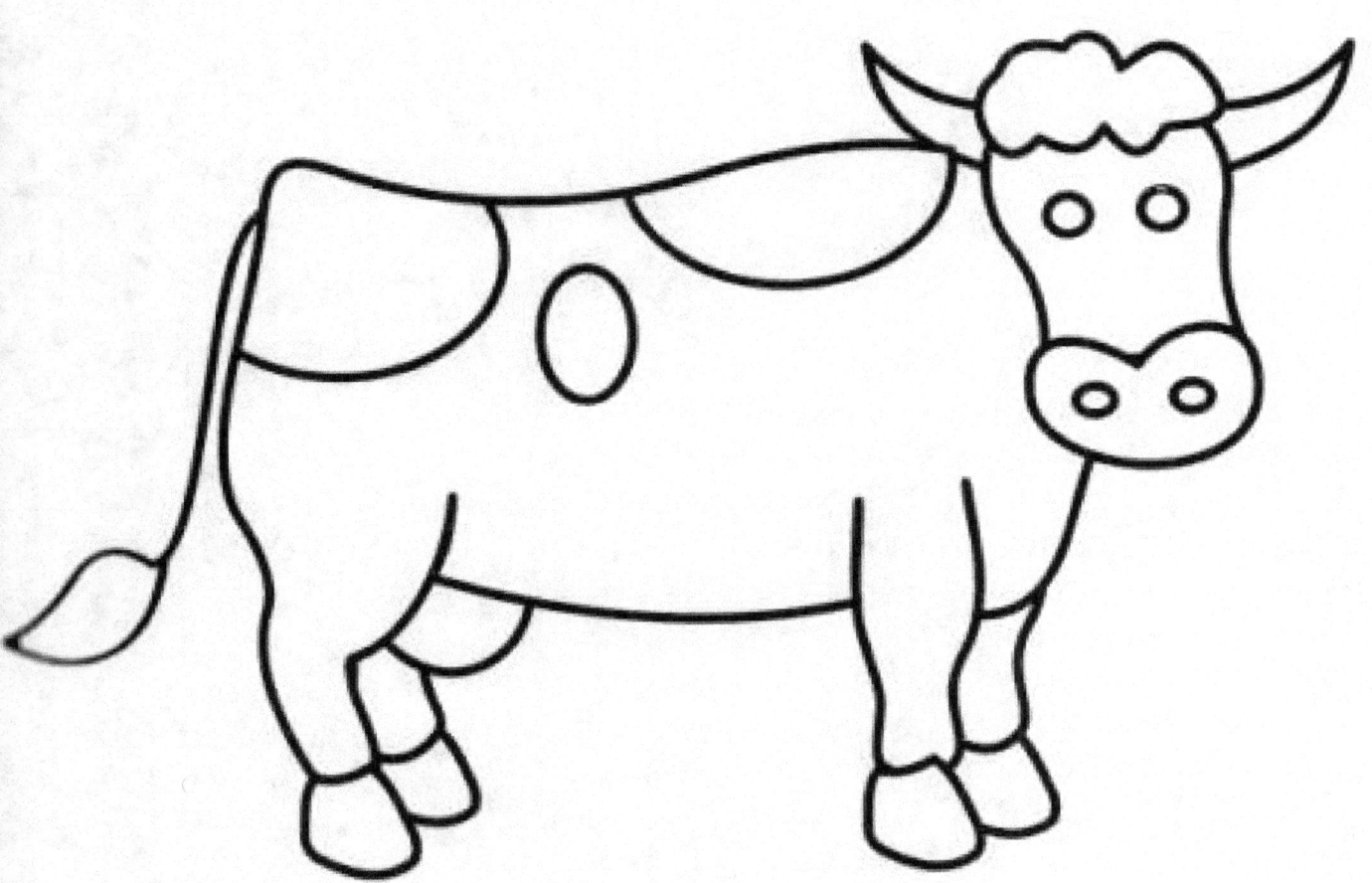

Horse - Caballo

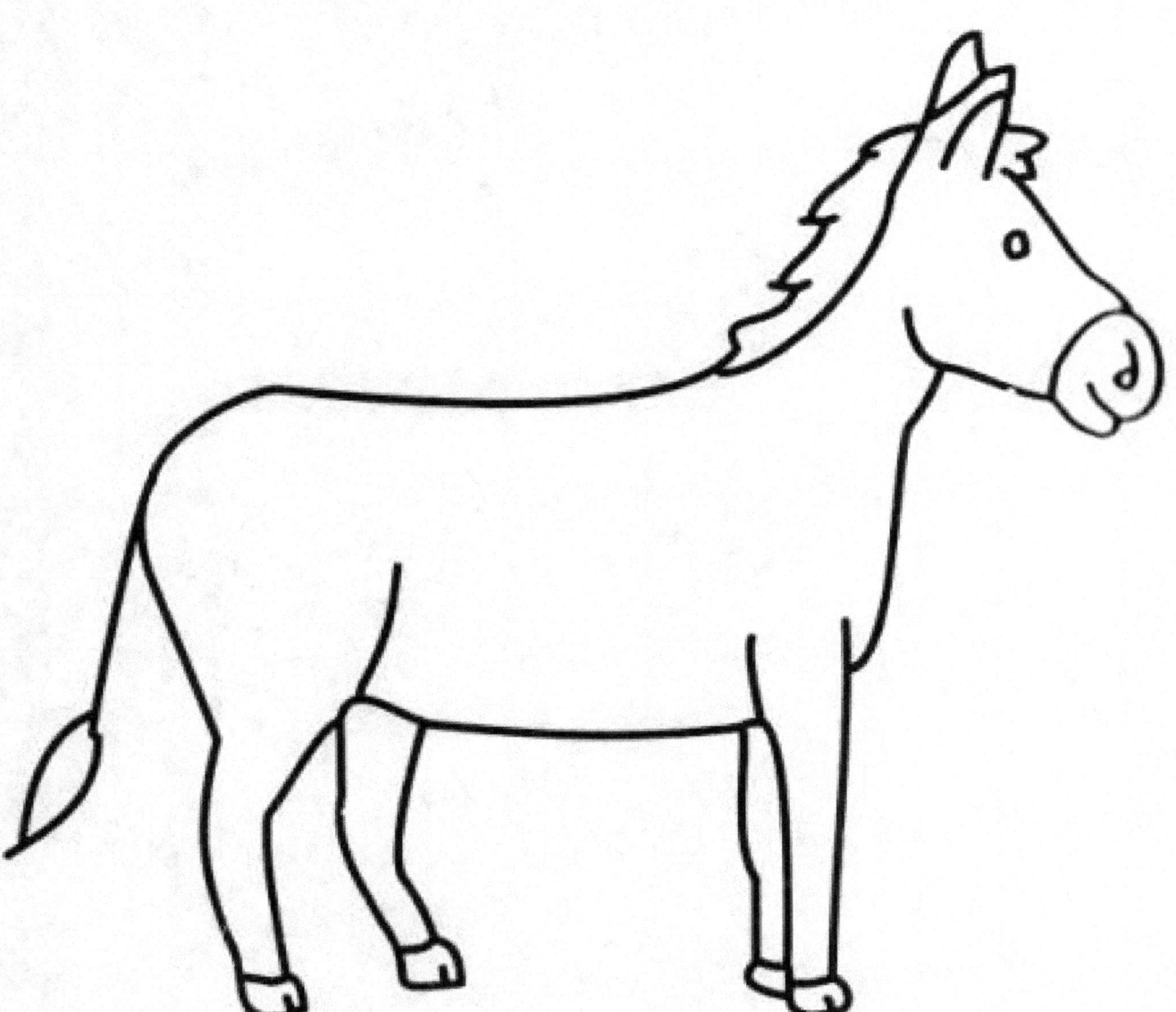

Sheep - Oveja

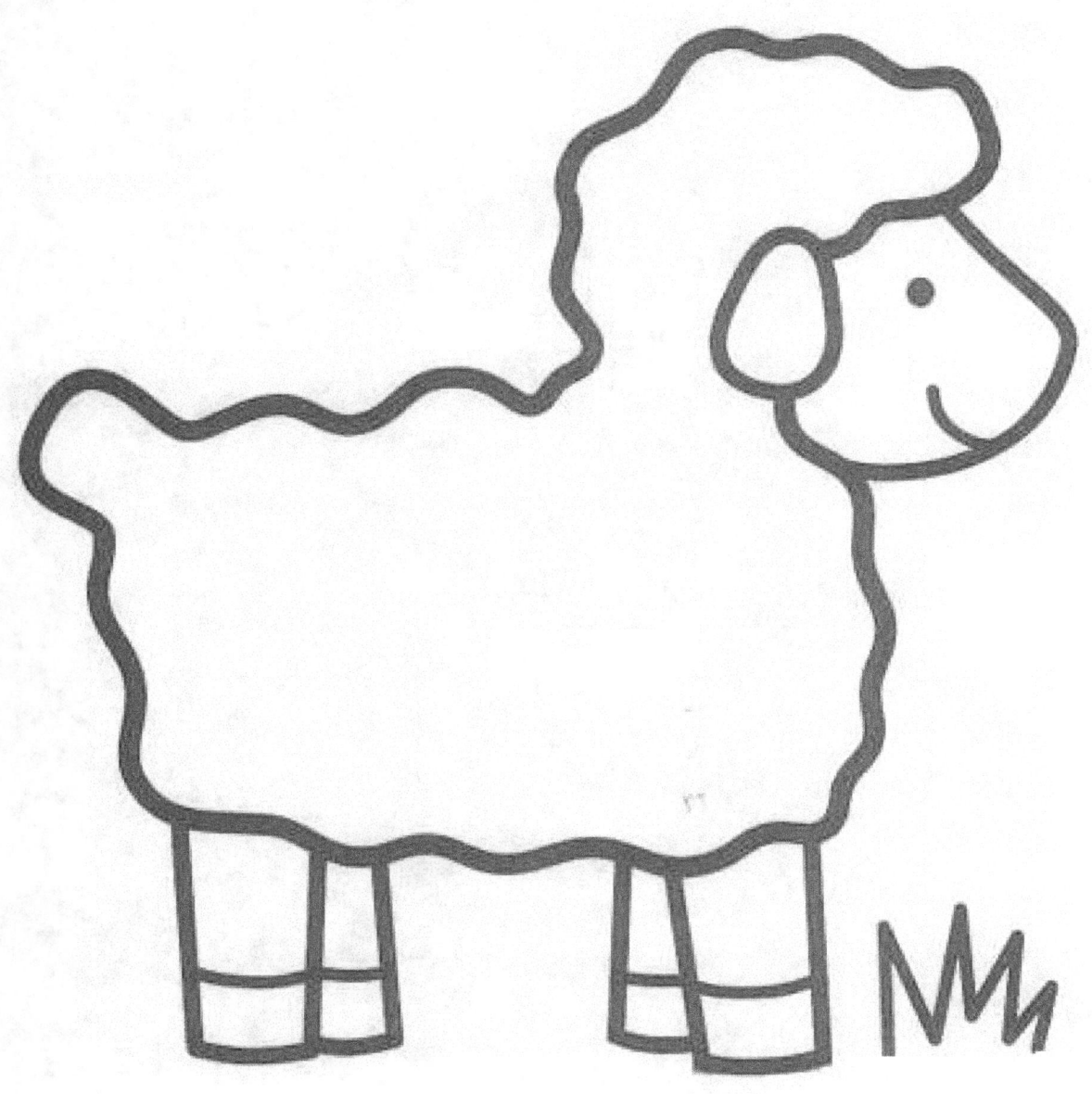

Rabbit - Conejo

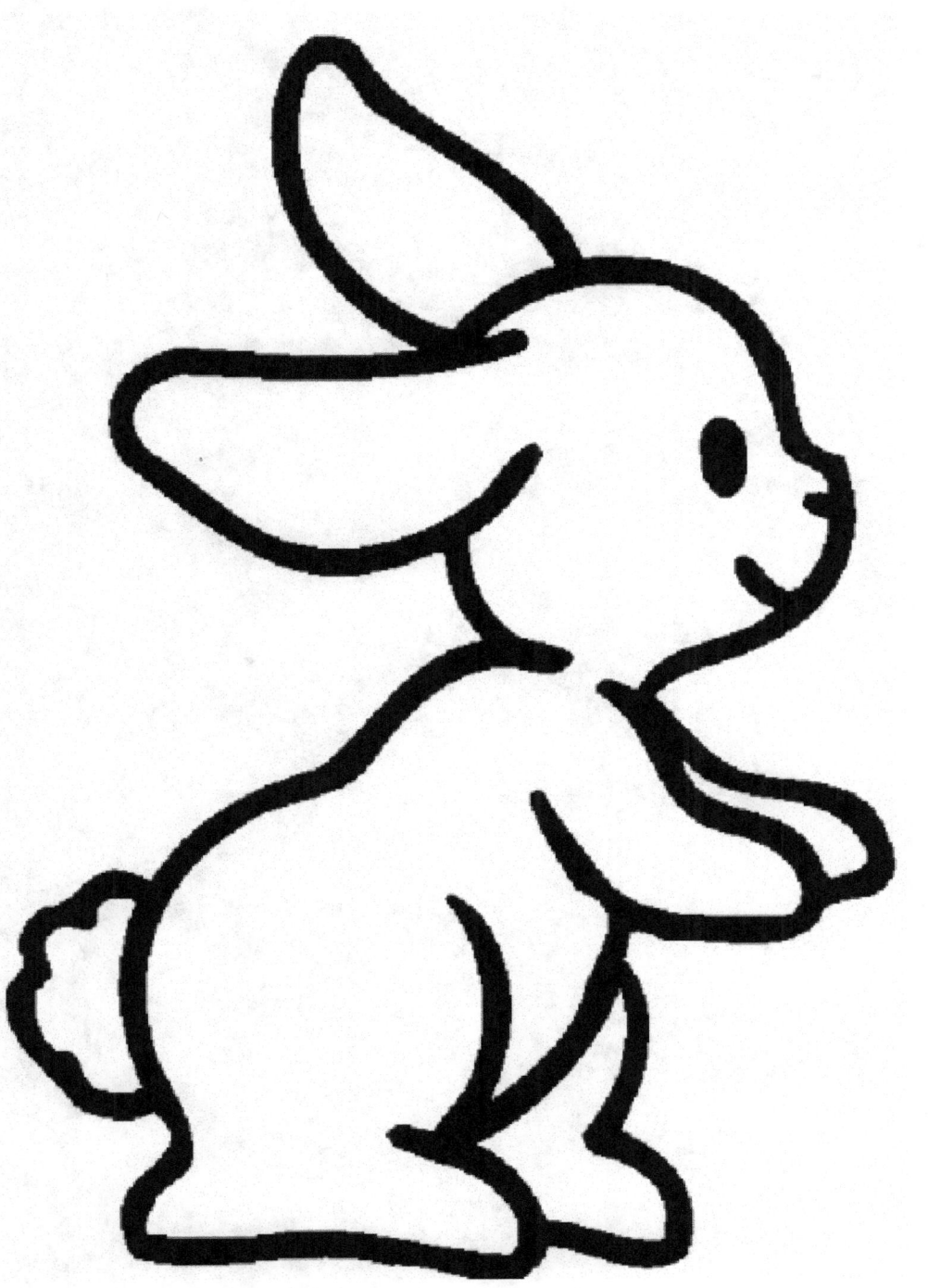

Squirrel - Ardilla

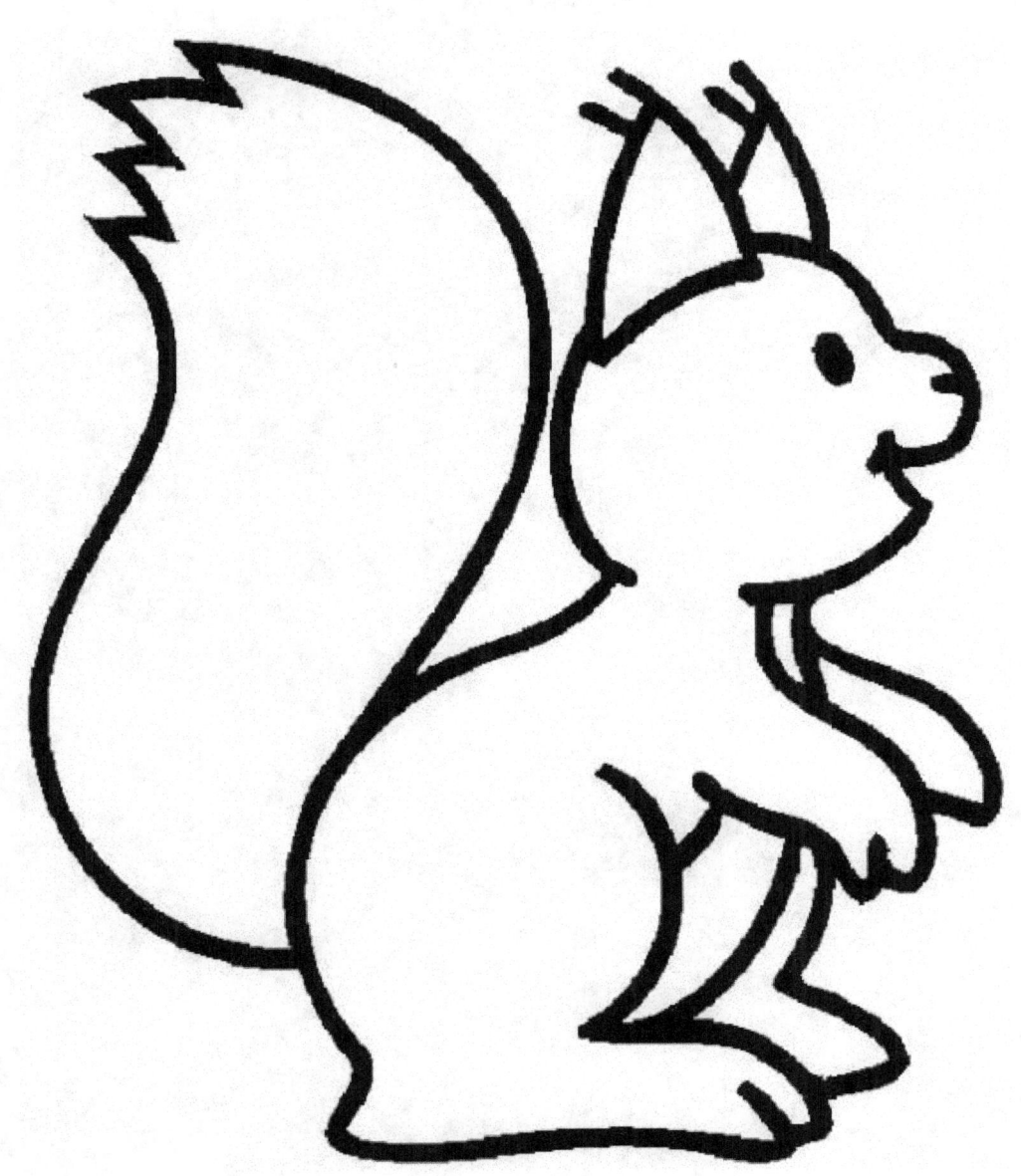

Mouse - Ratón

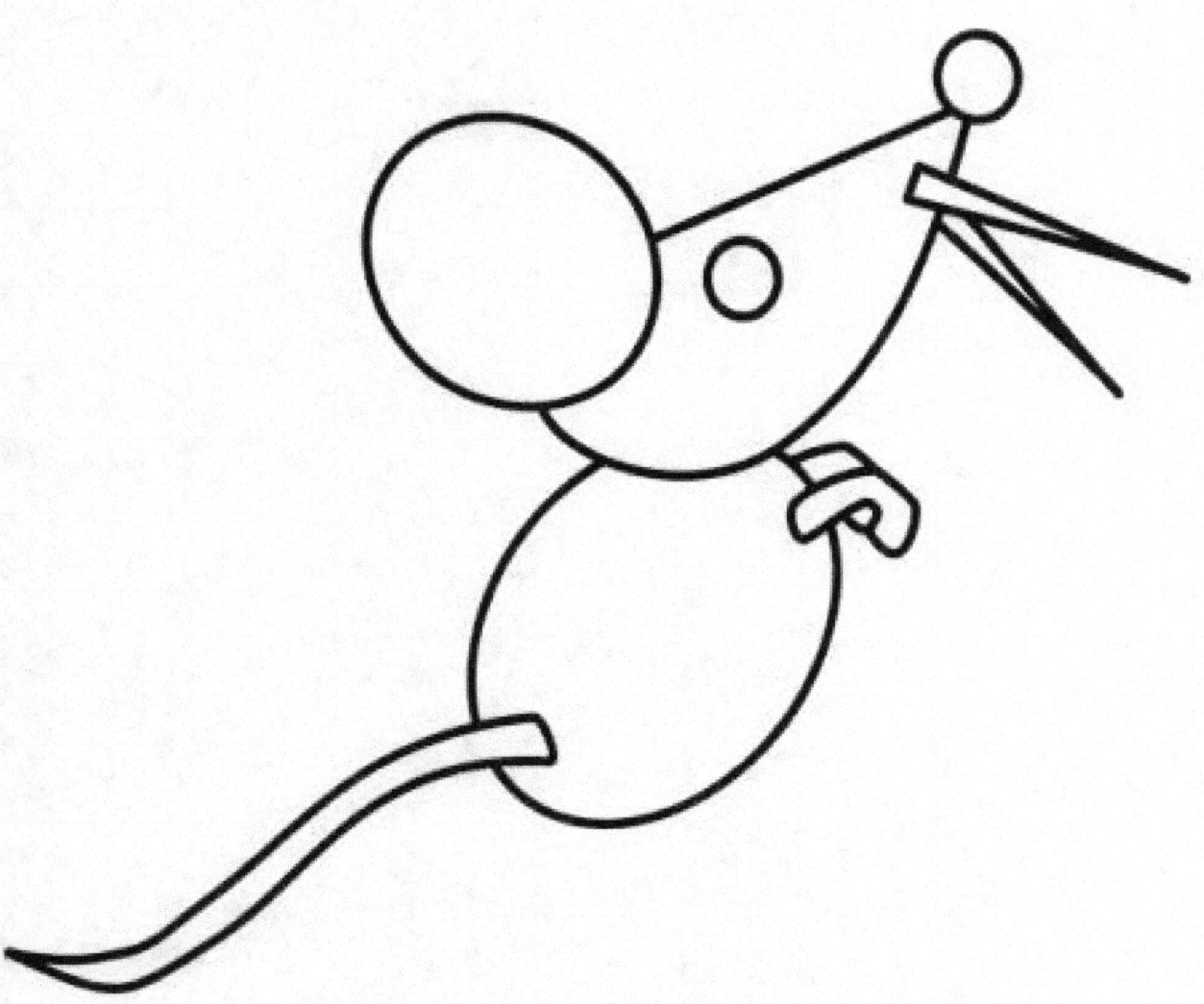

Worm - Gusano

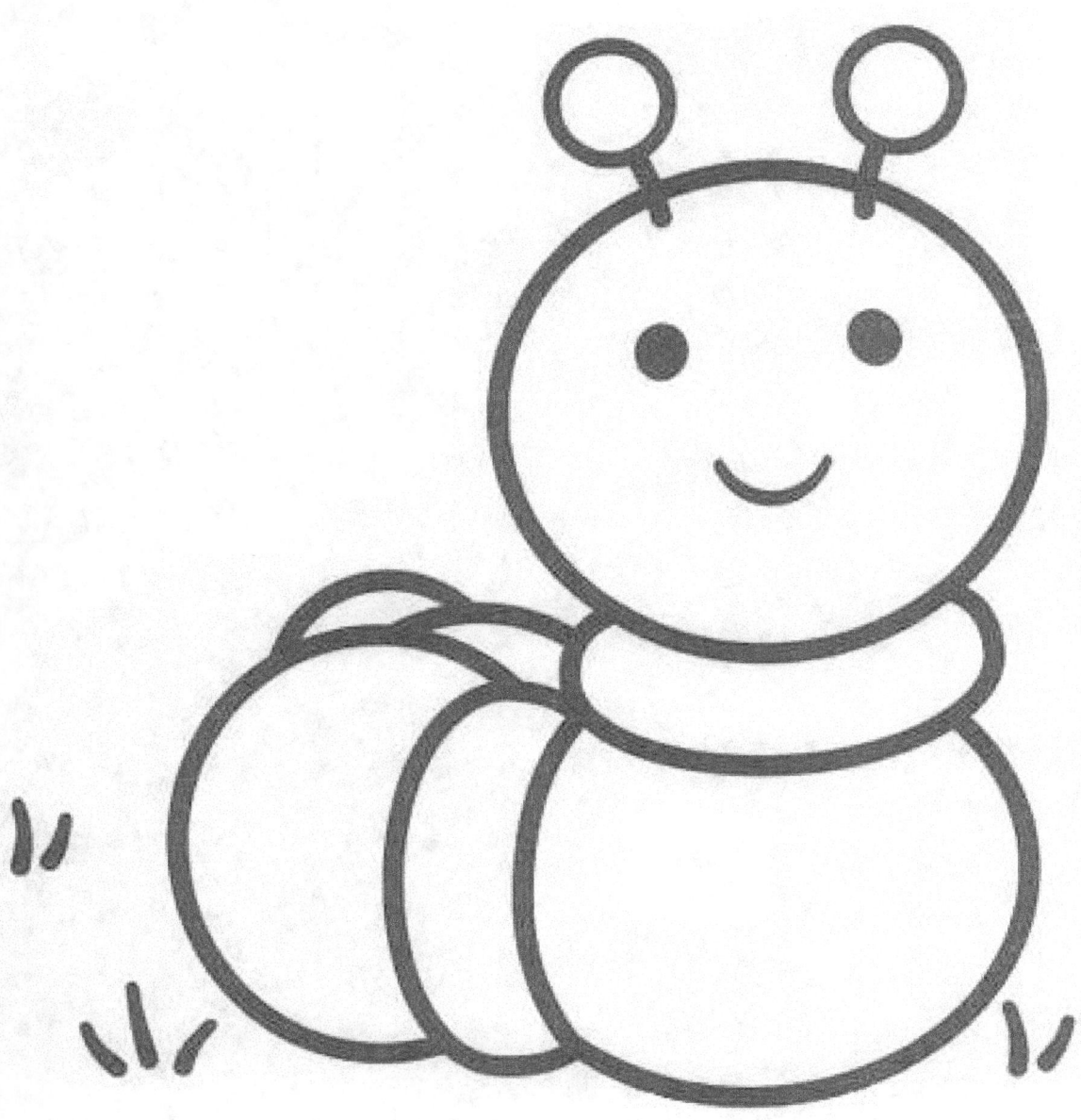

Bee - Abeja

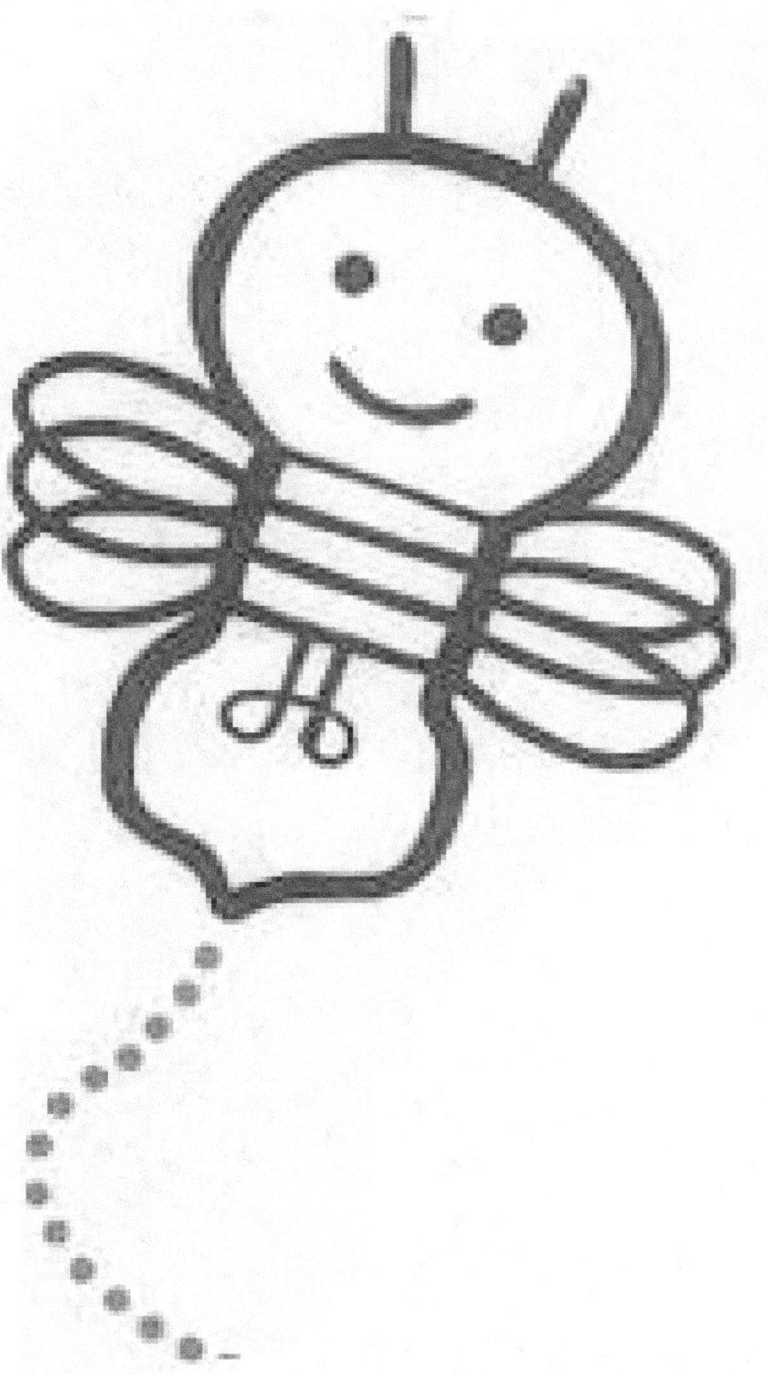

Butterfly - Mariposa

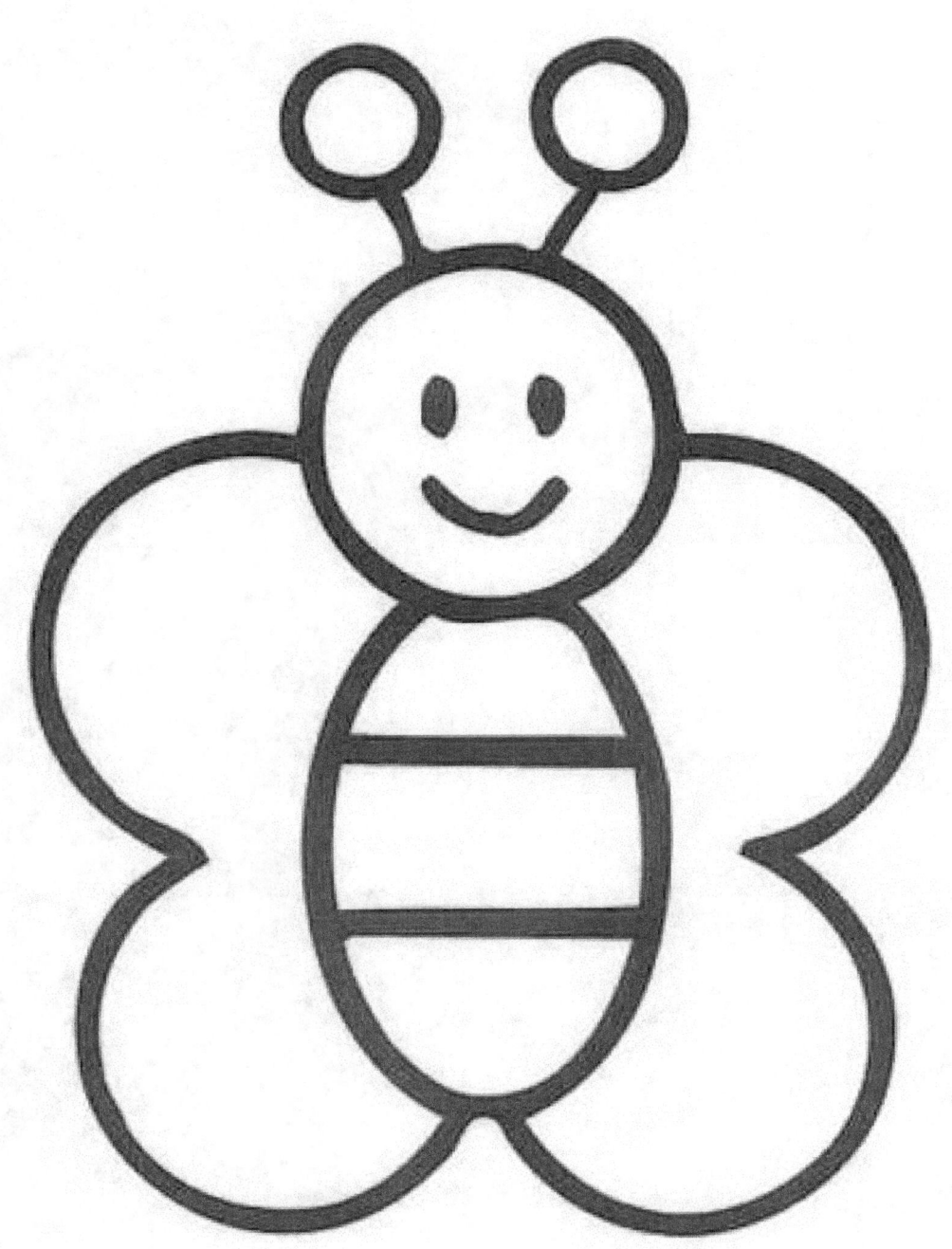

Ant - Hormiga

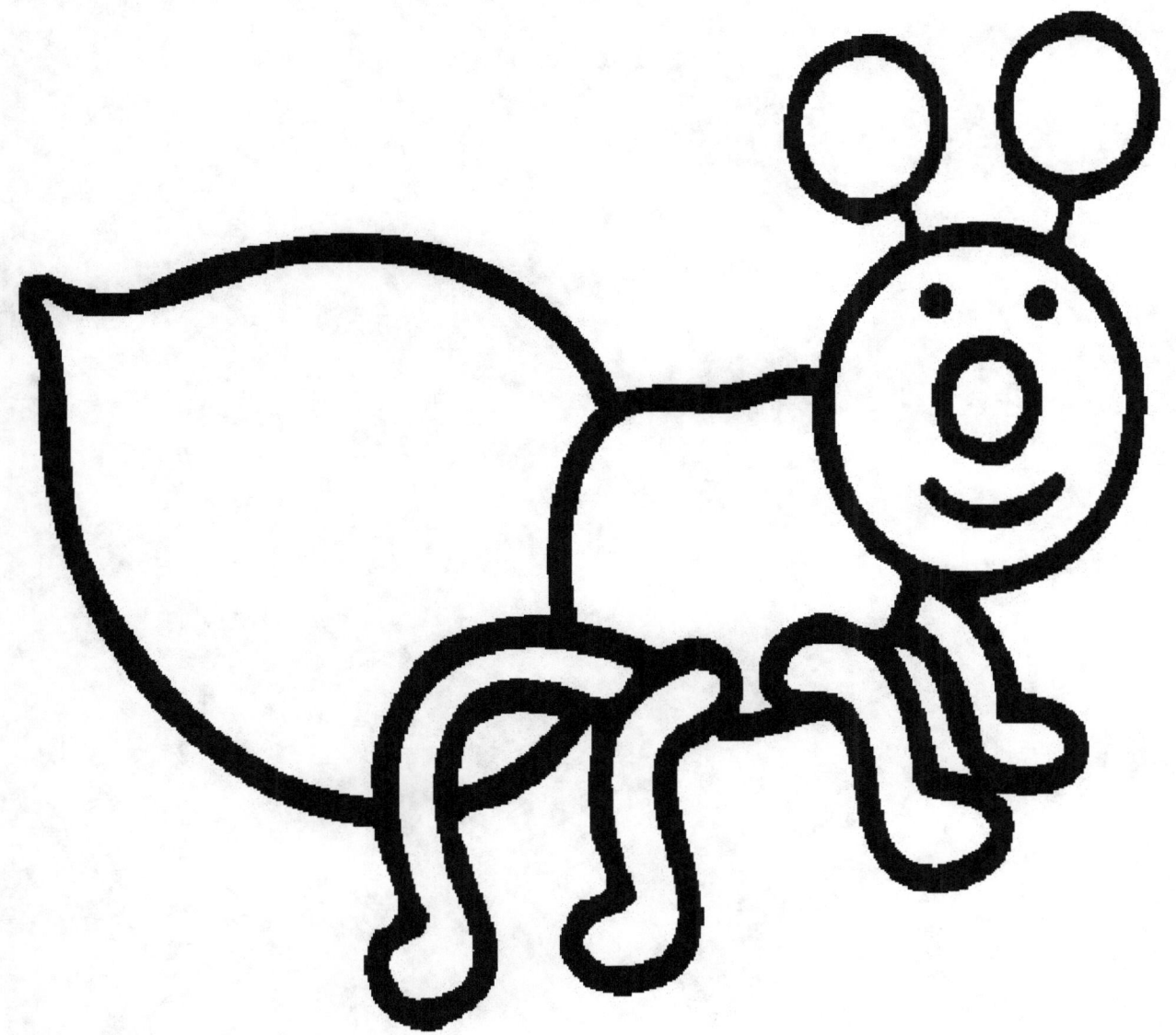

Ladybugs - Mariquitas

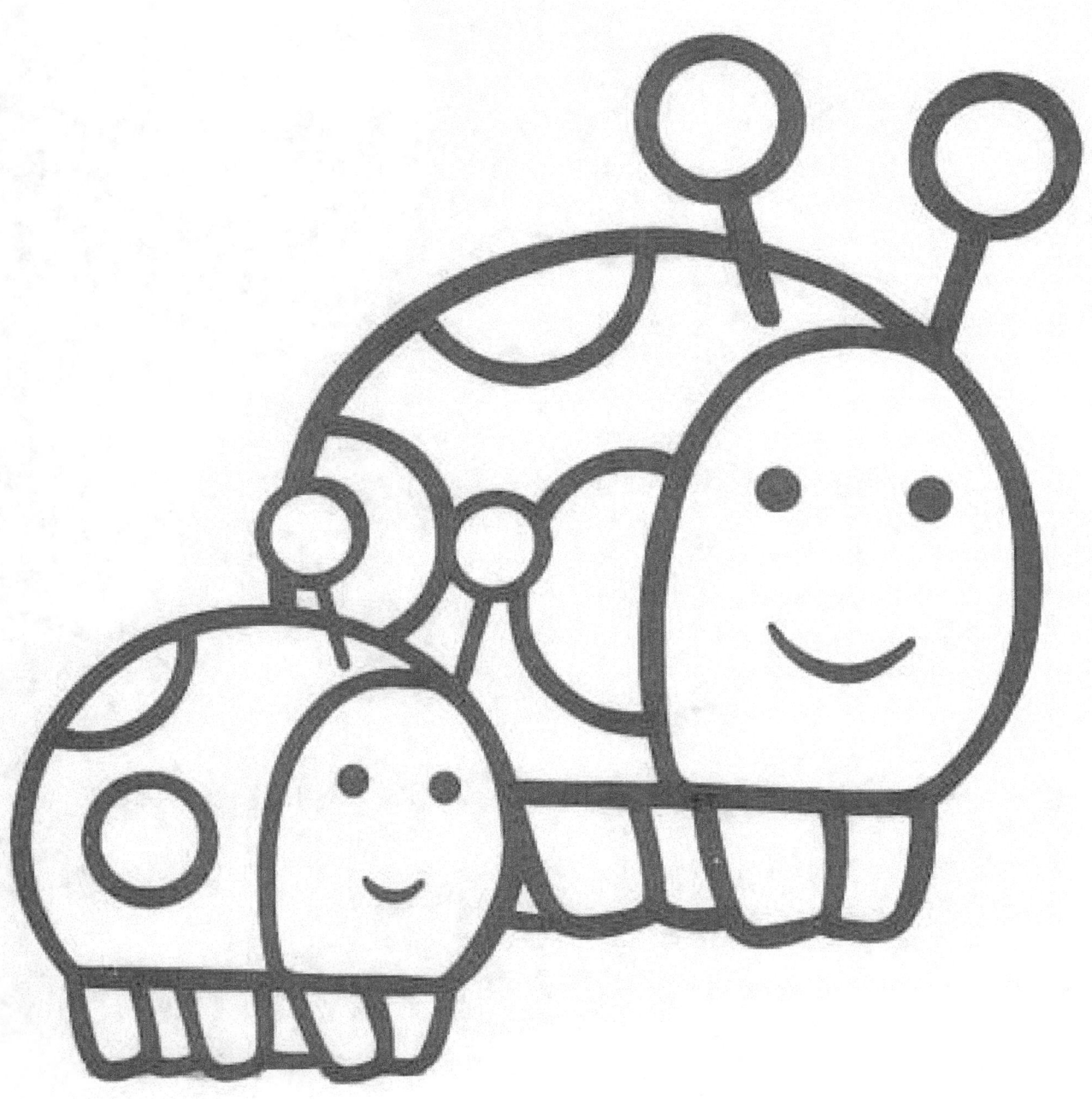

Spider - Araña

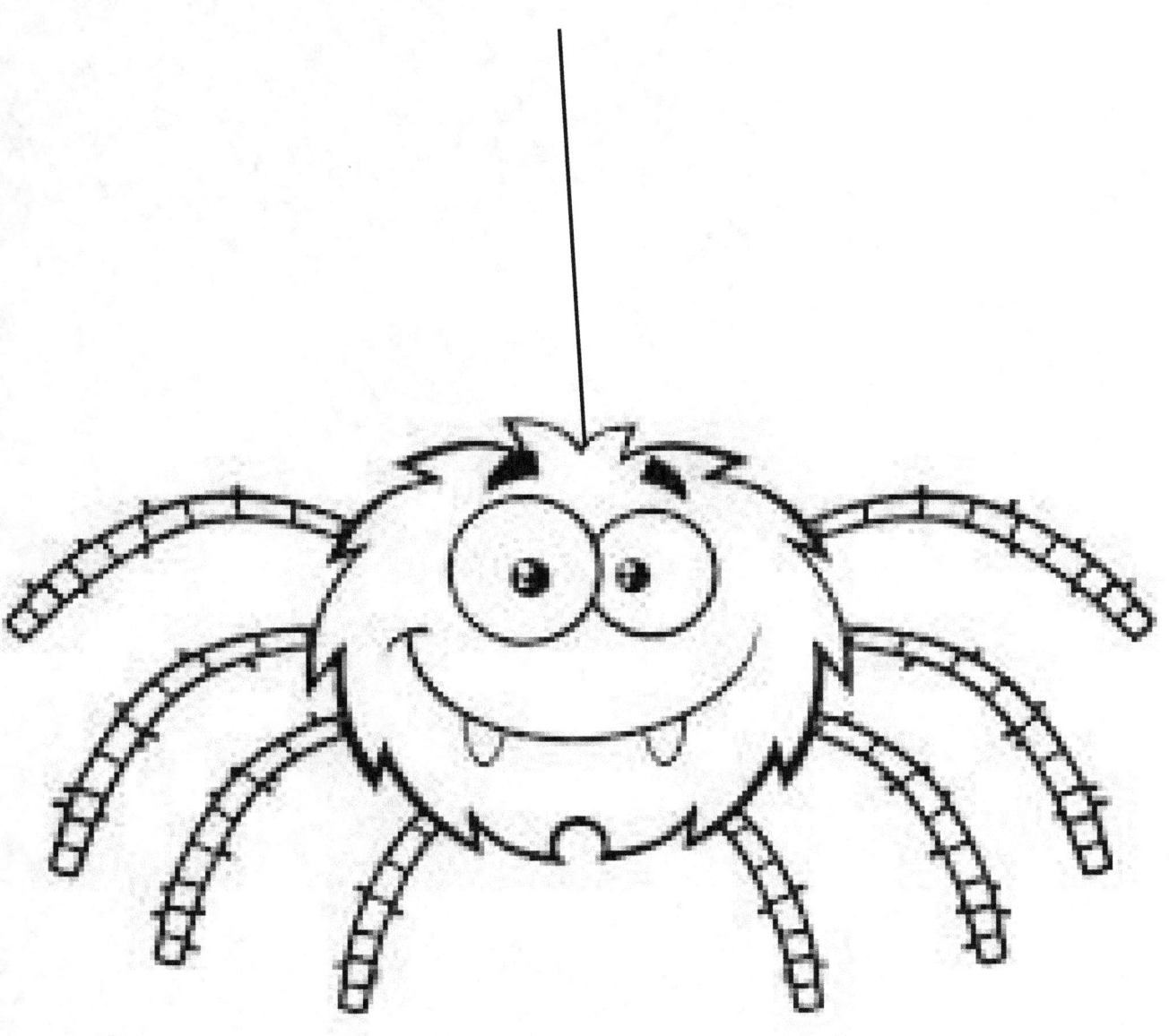

Snail - Caracol

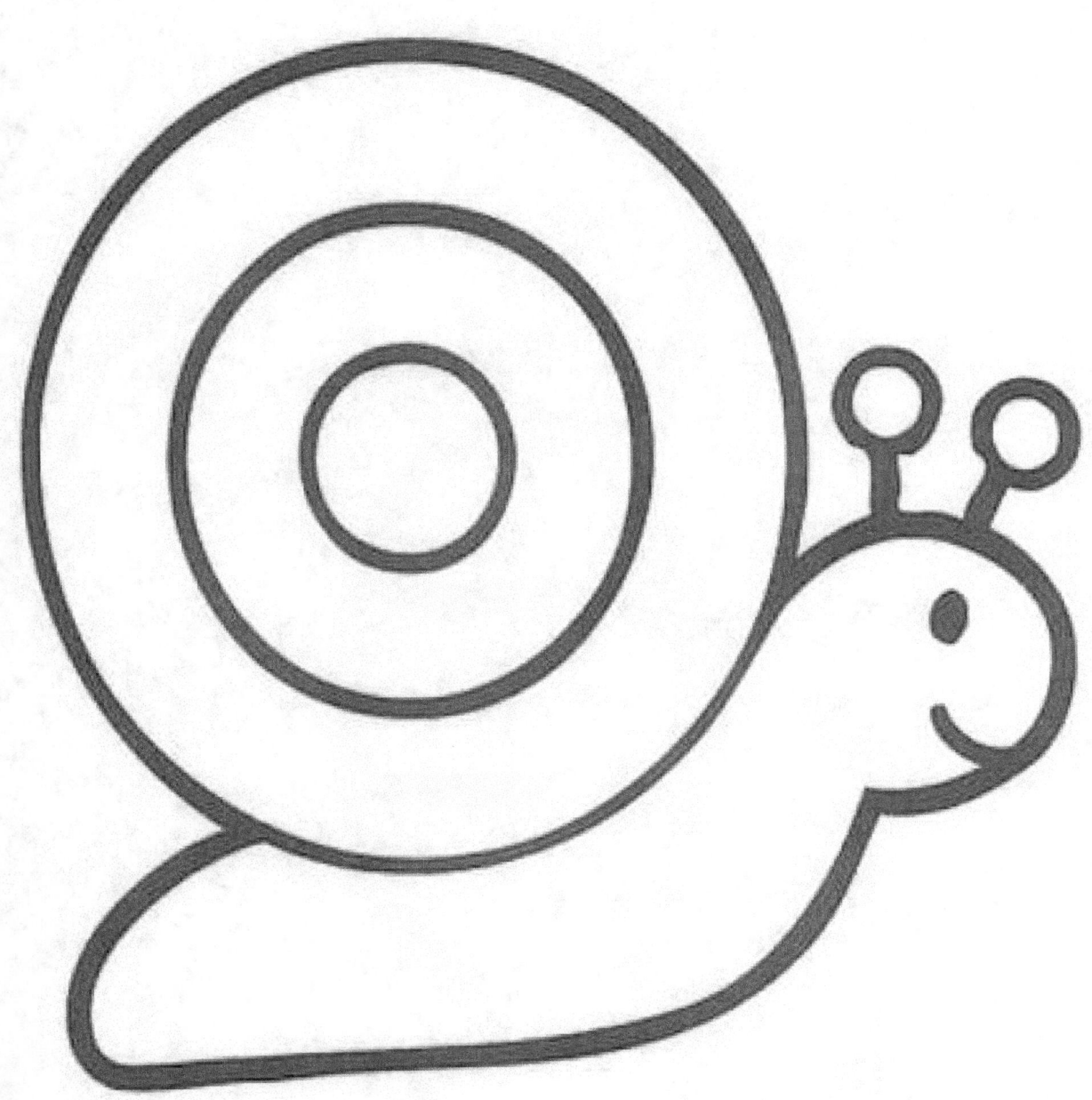

Parrot - Loro

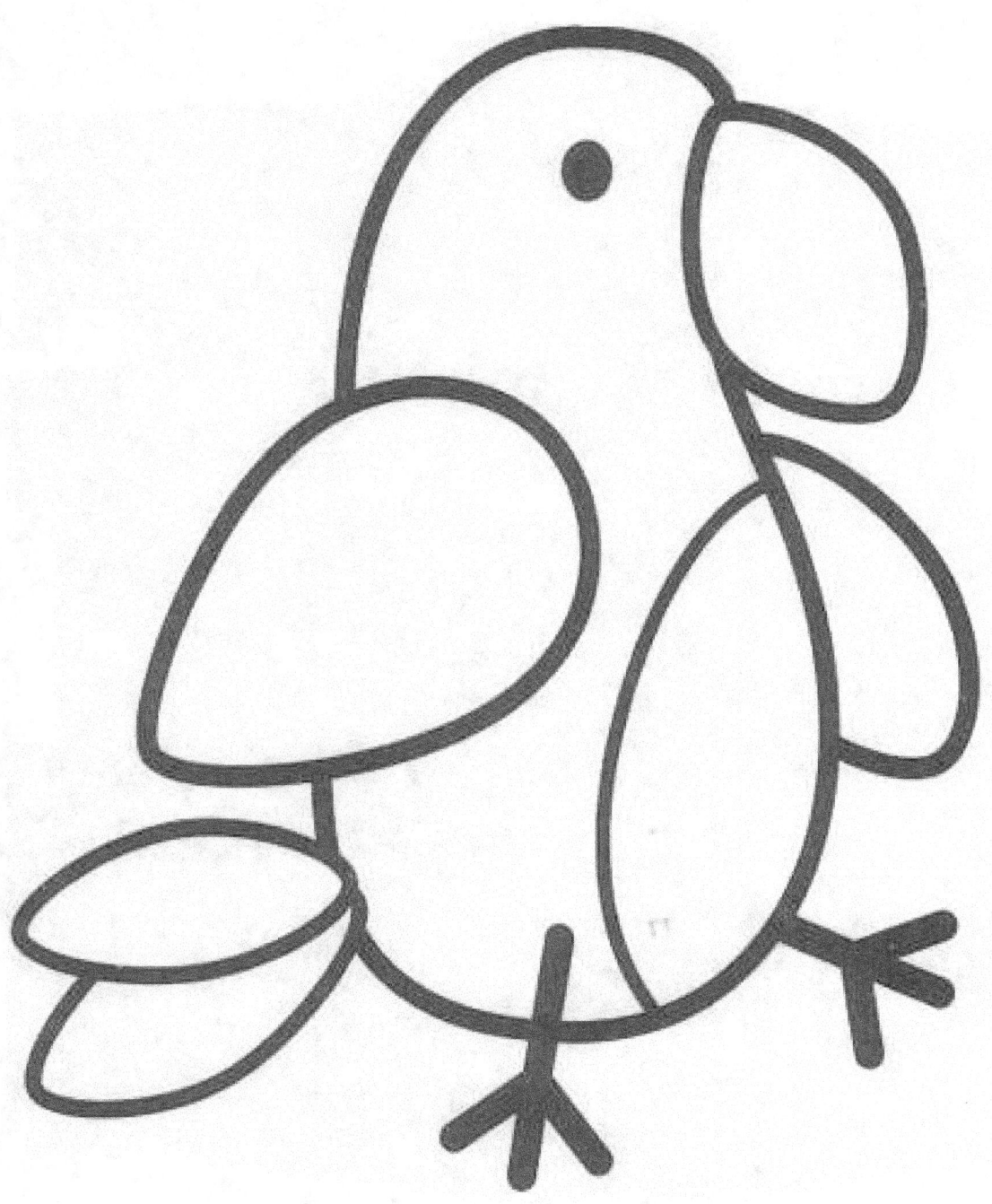

Owl - Búho

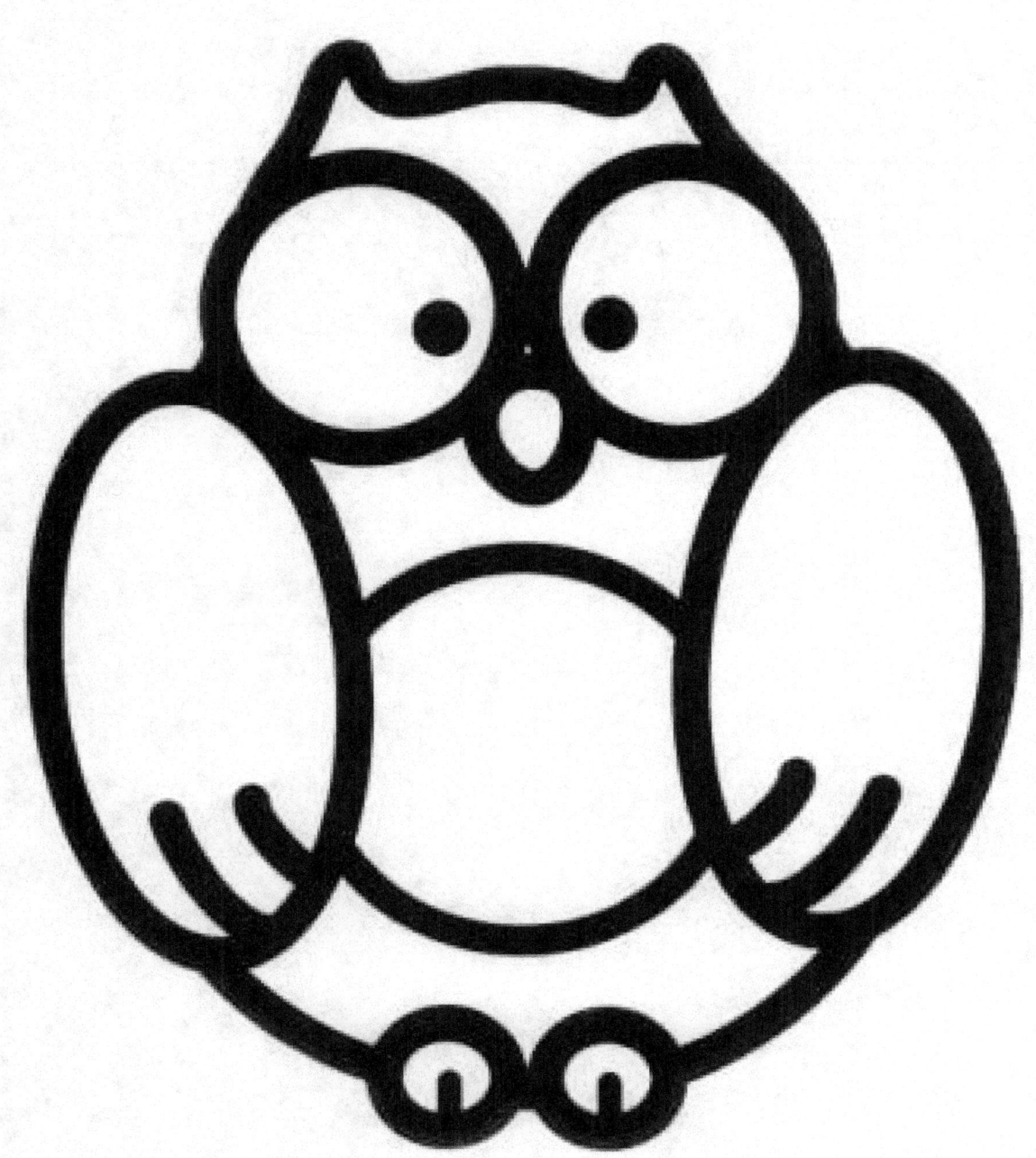

Bird - Pájaro

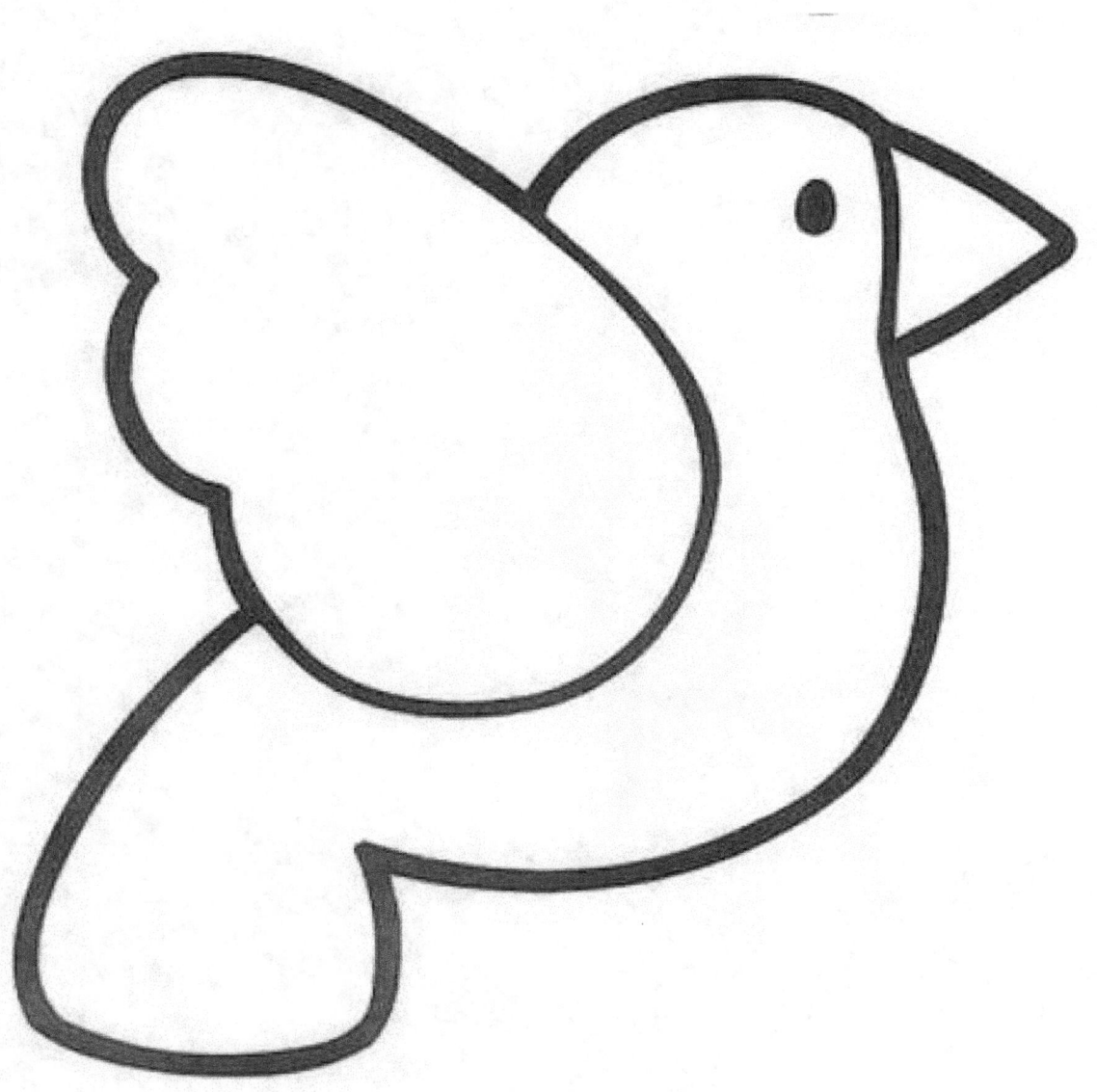

Frog - Rana

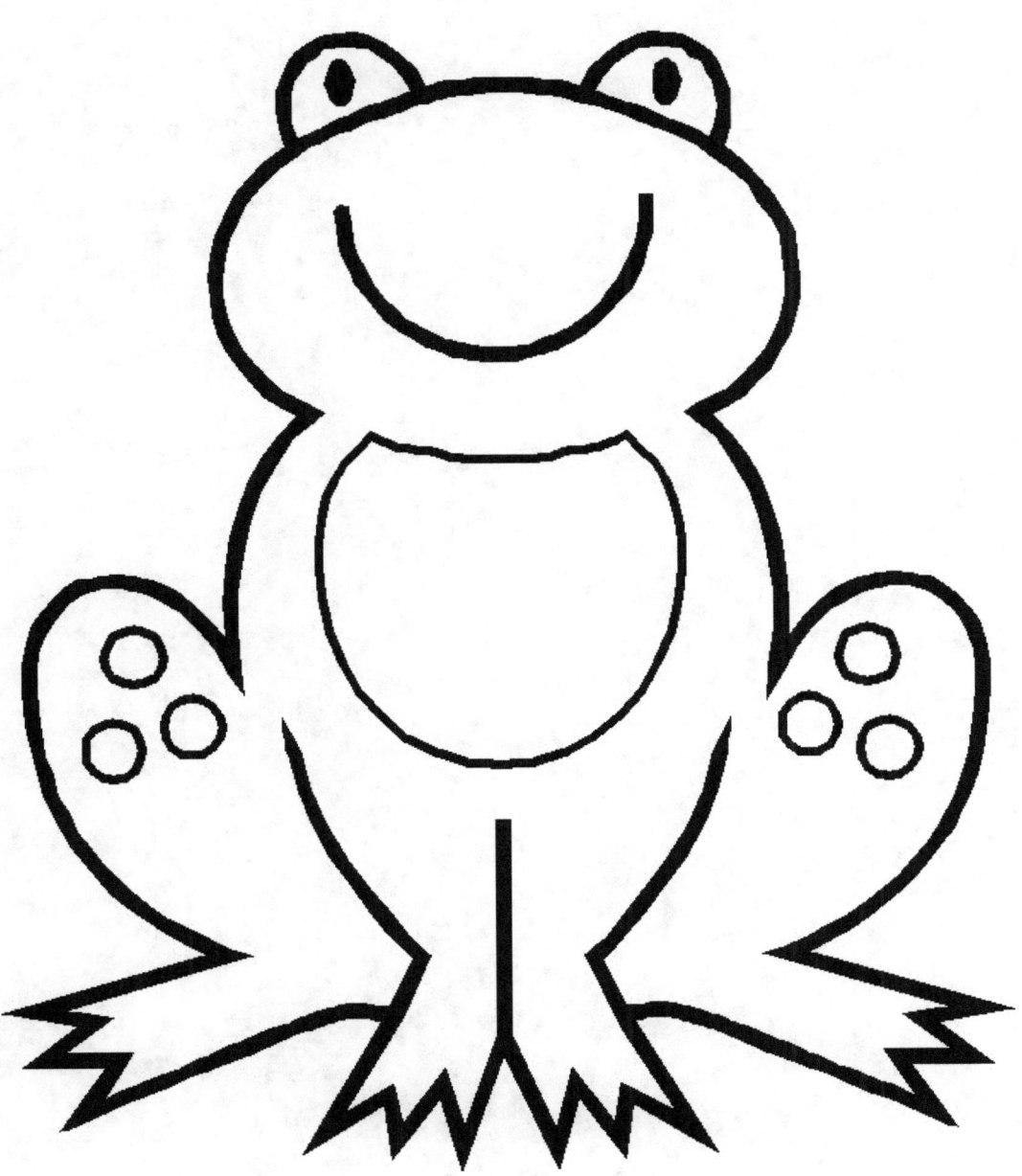

Turtle - Tortuga

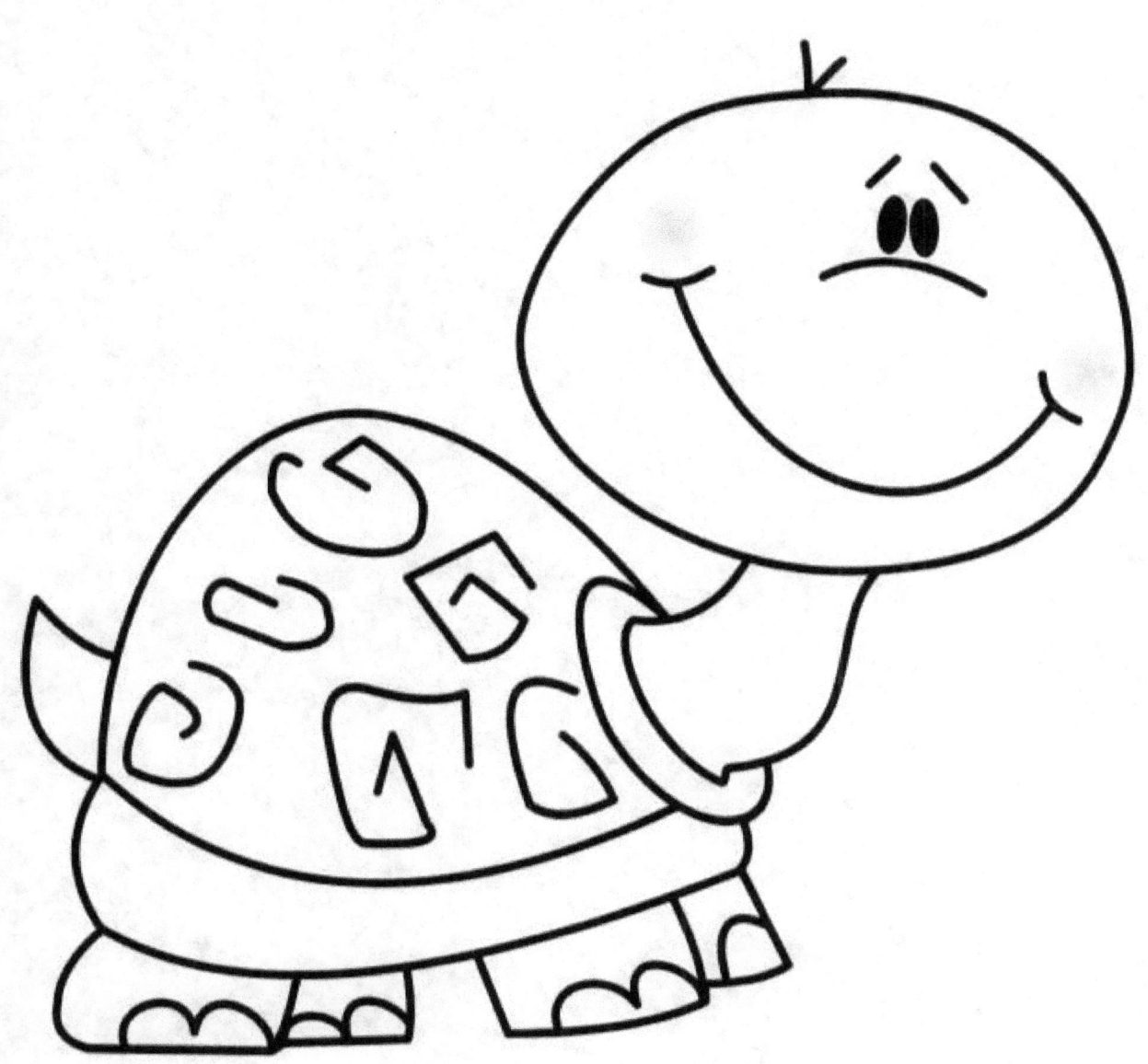

Seal - Foca

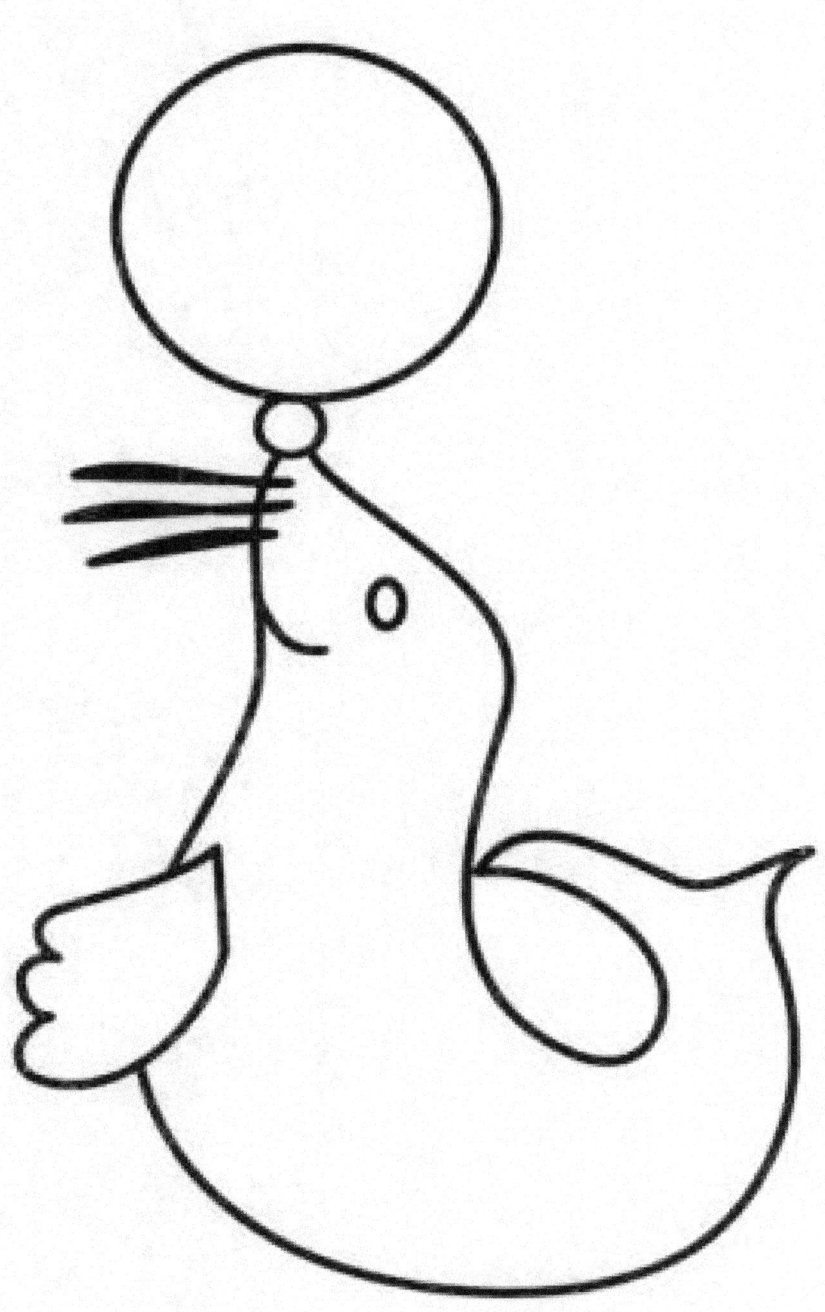

Fish - Pez

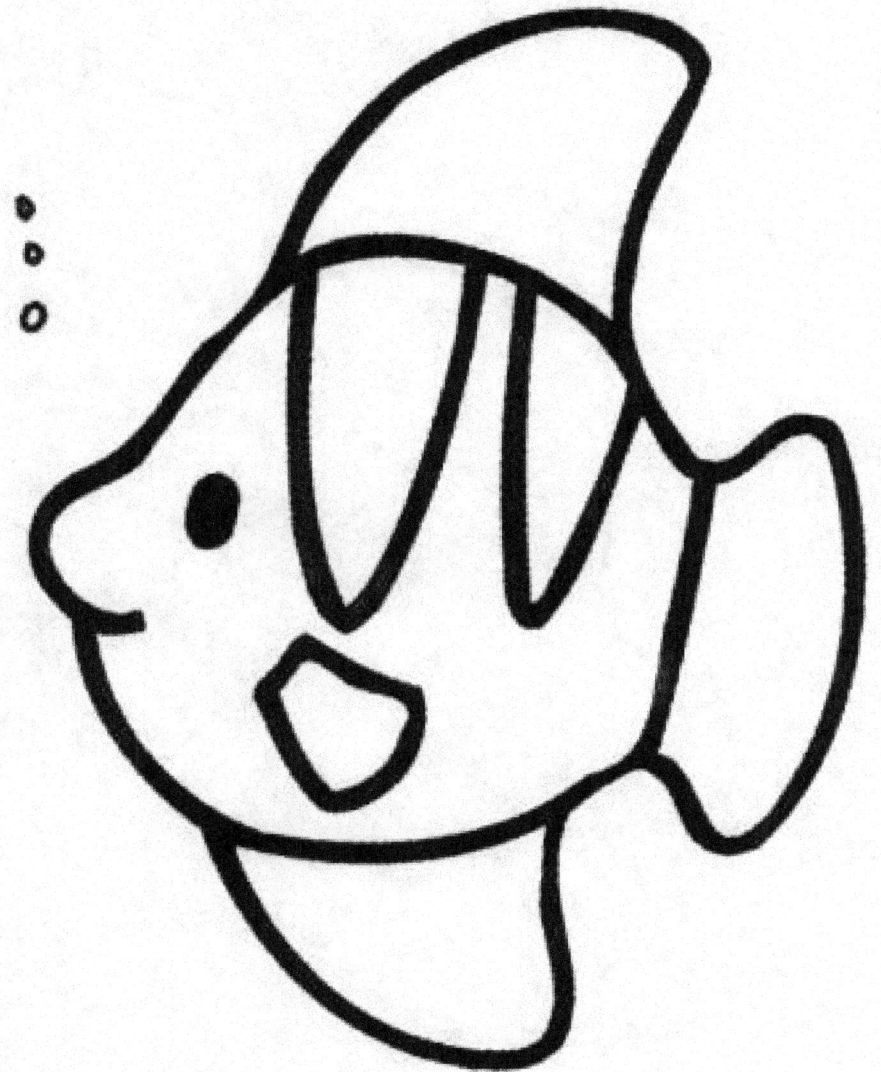

Octopus - Pulpo

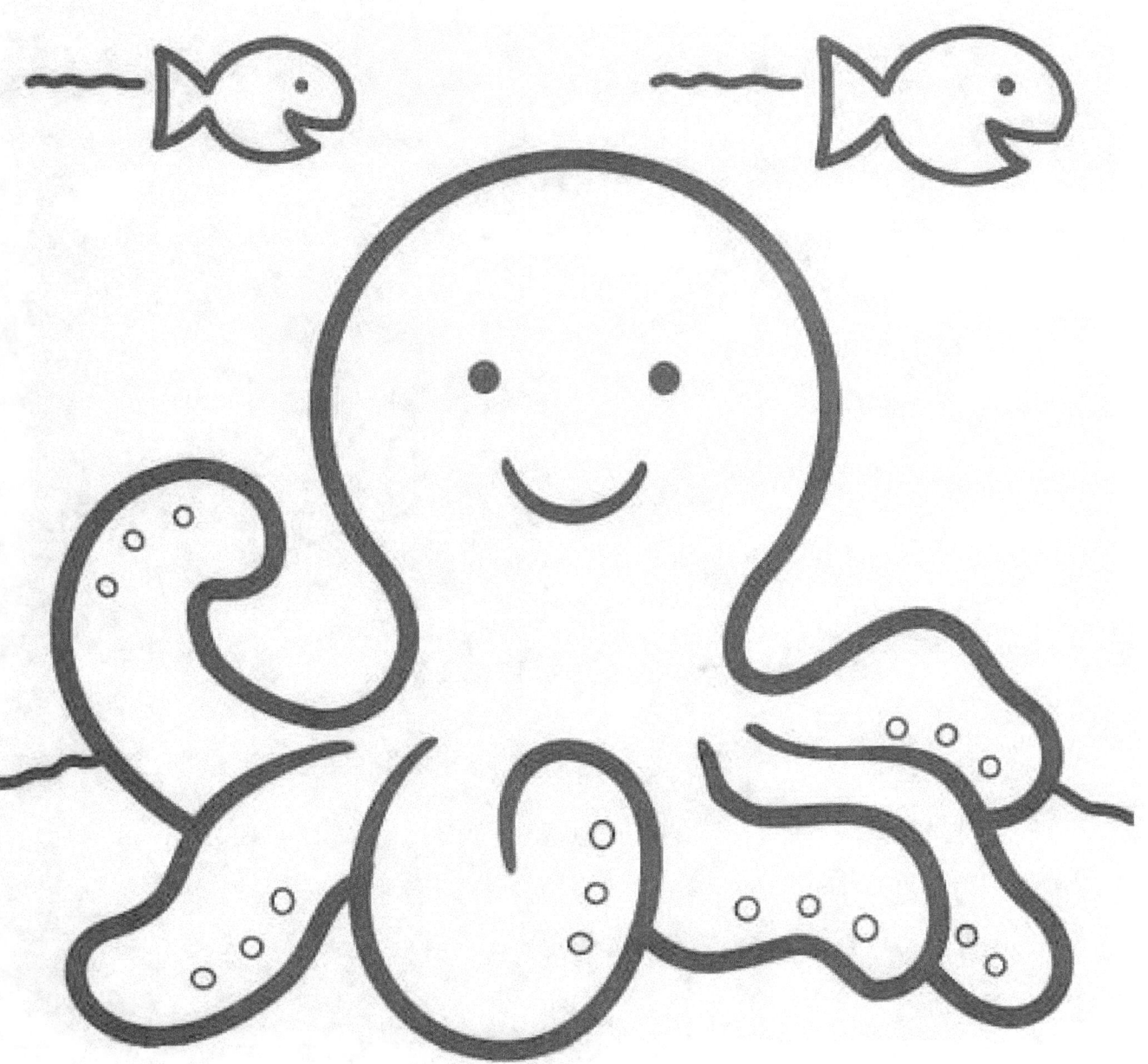

Whale - Ballena

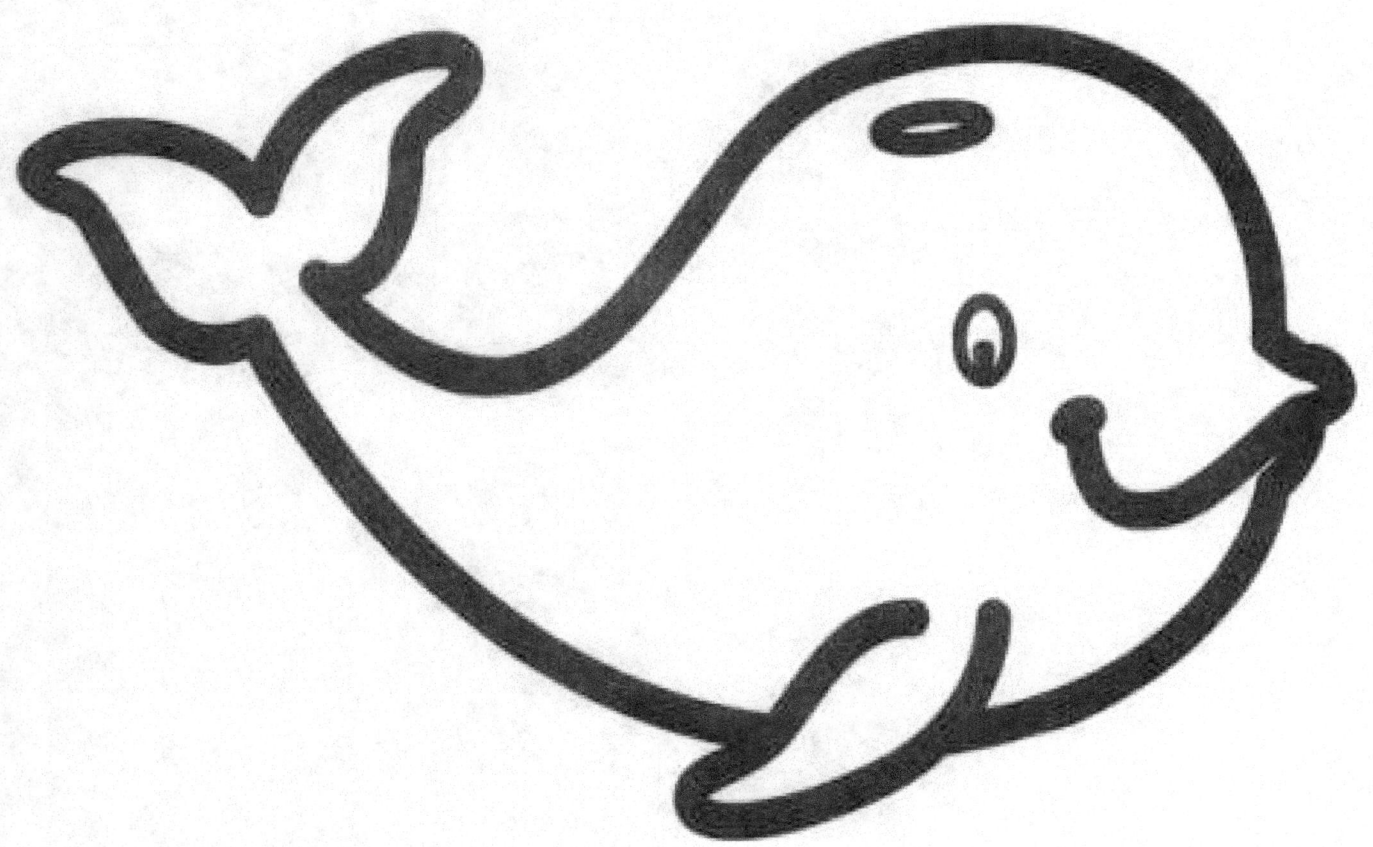

Squid - Calamar

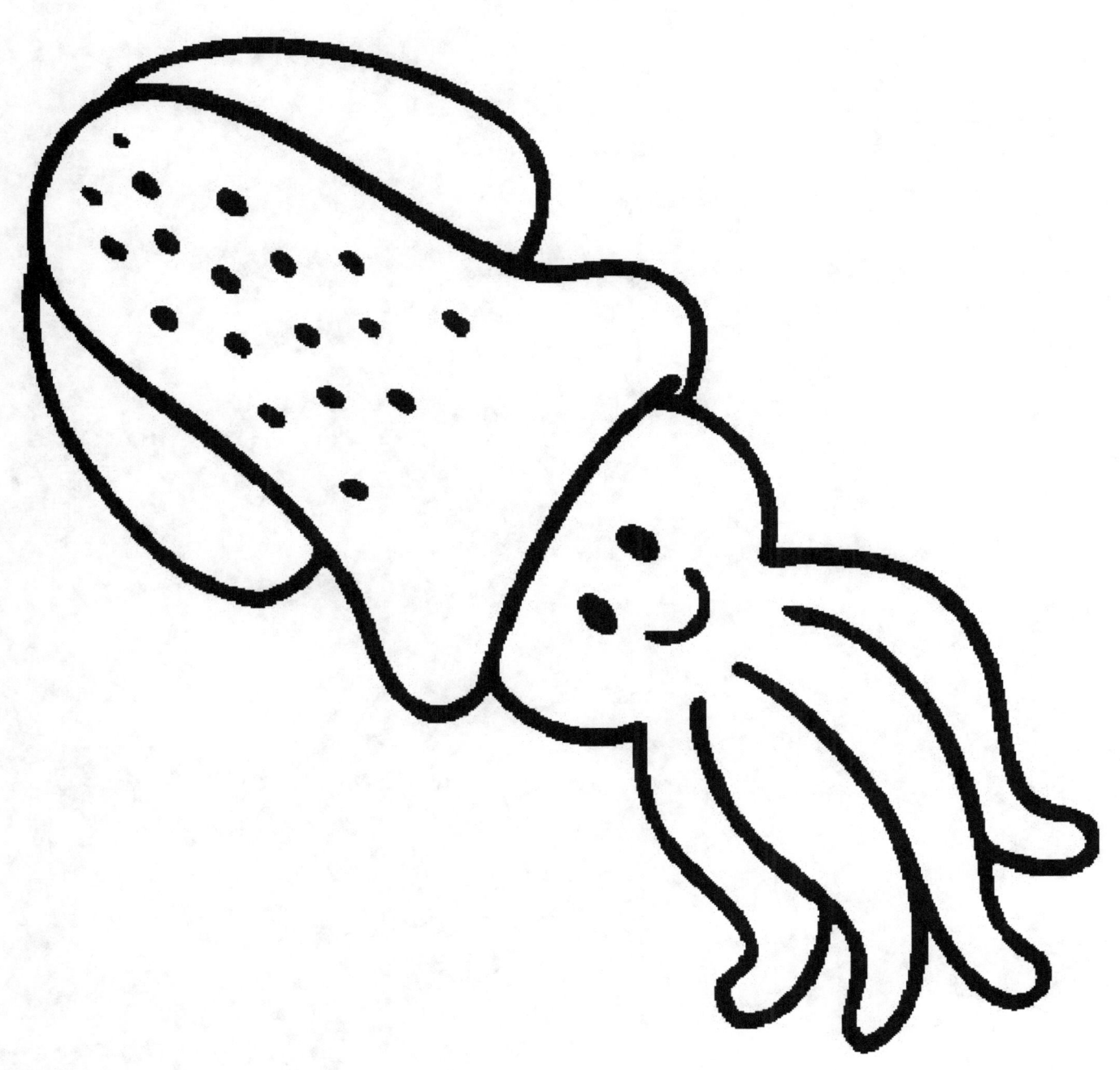

Clam - Almeja

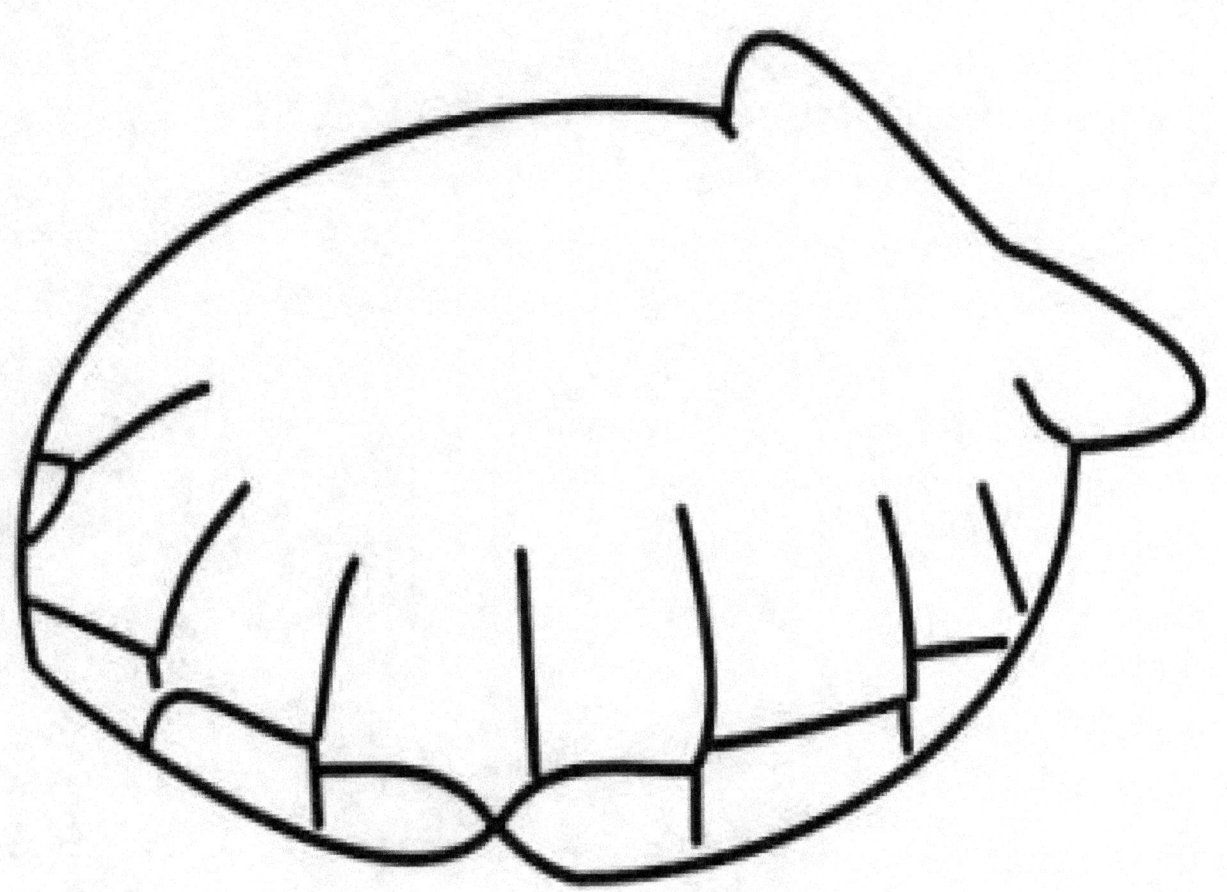

Crab - Cangrejo

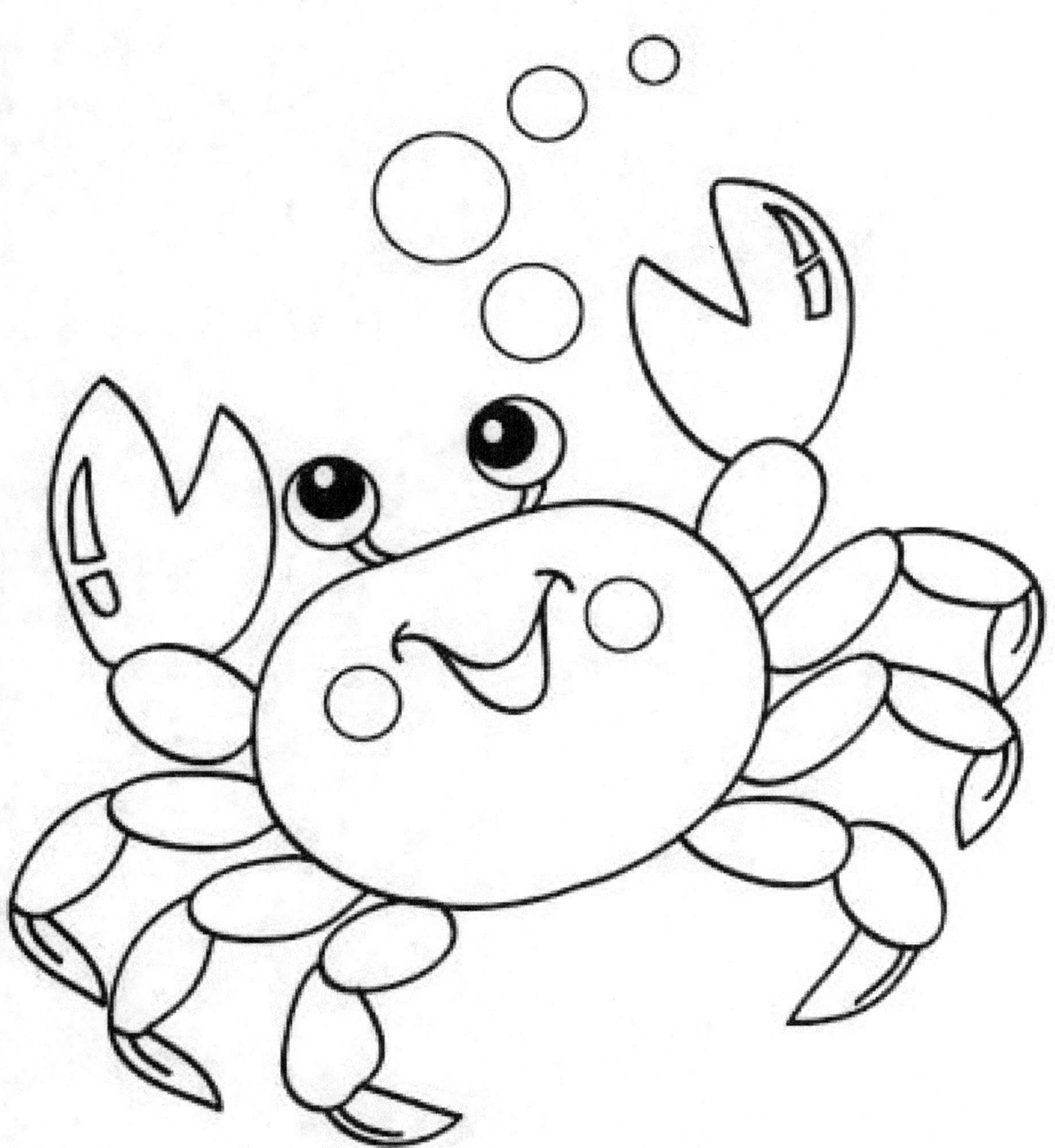

Starfish – Estrella de mar

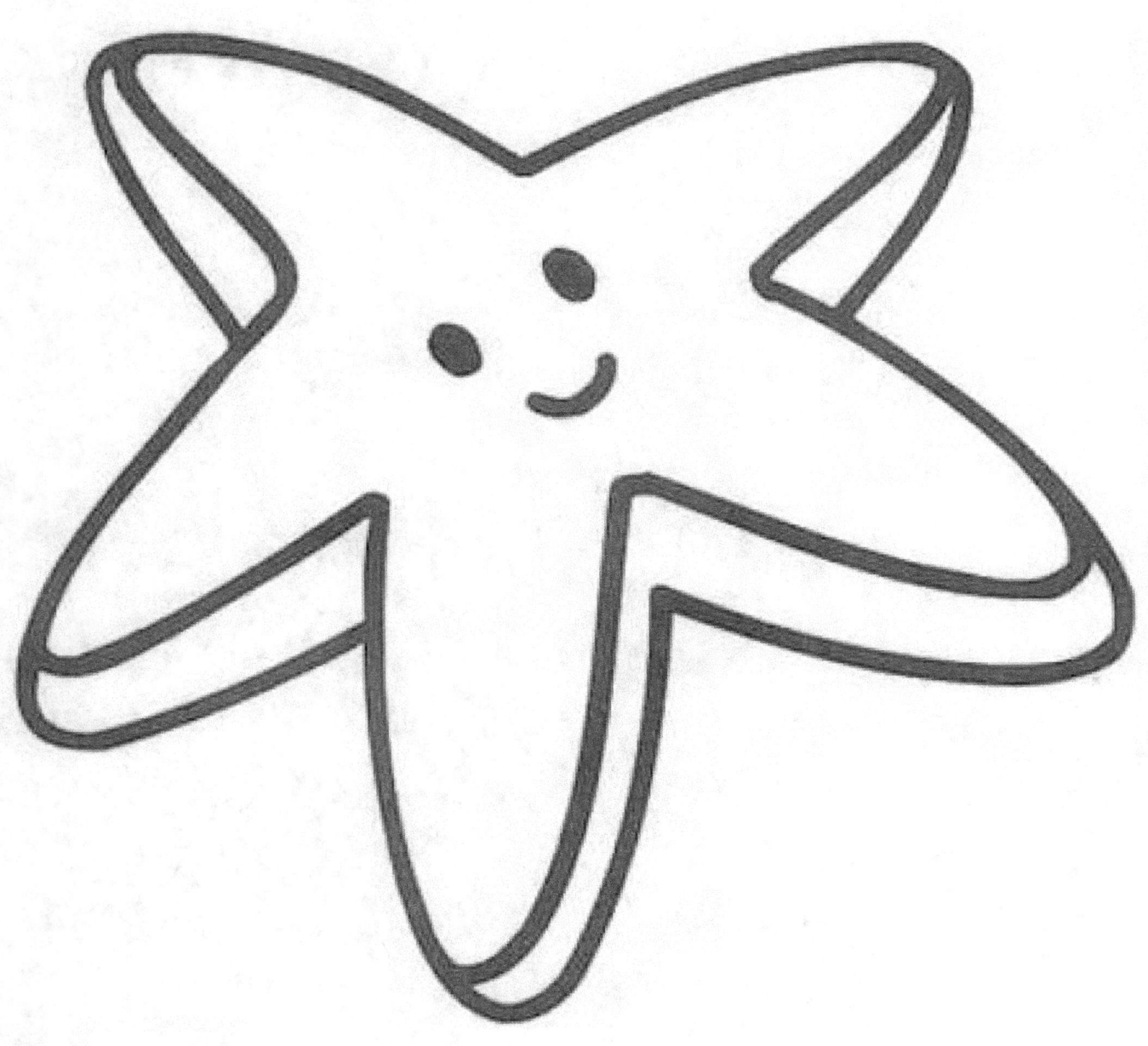

Hippopotamus - Hipopótamo

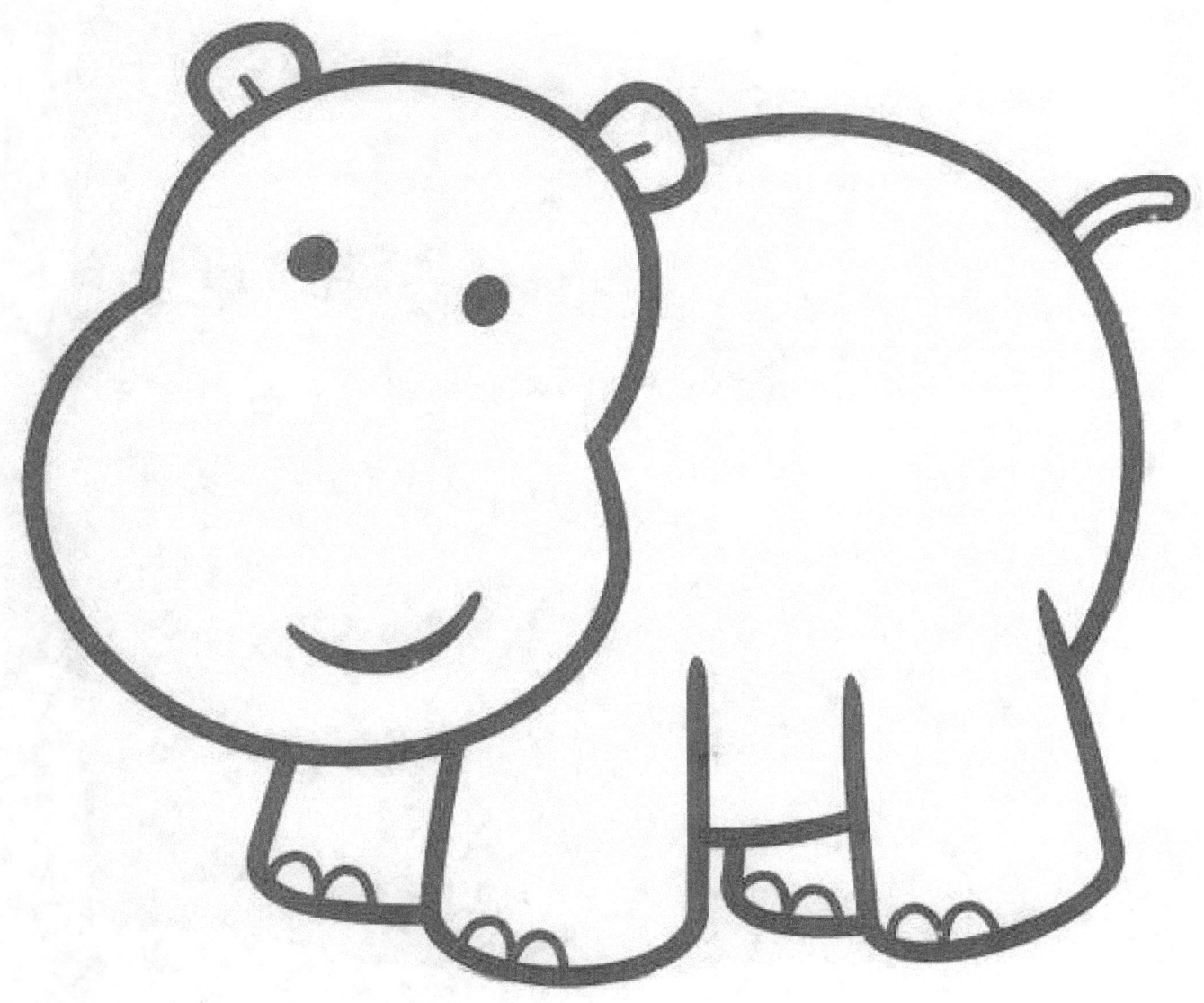

Crocodile - Cocodrilo

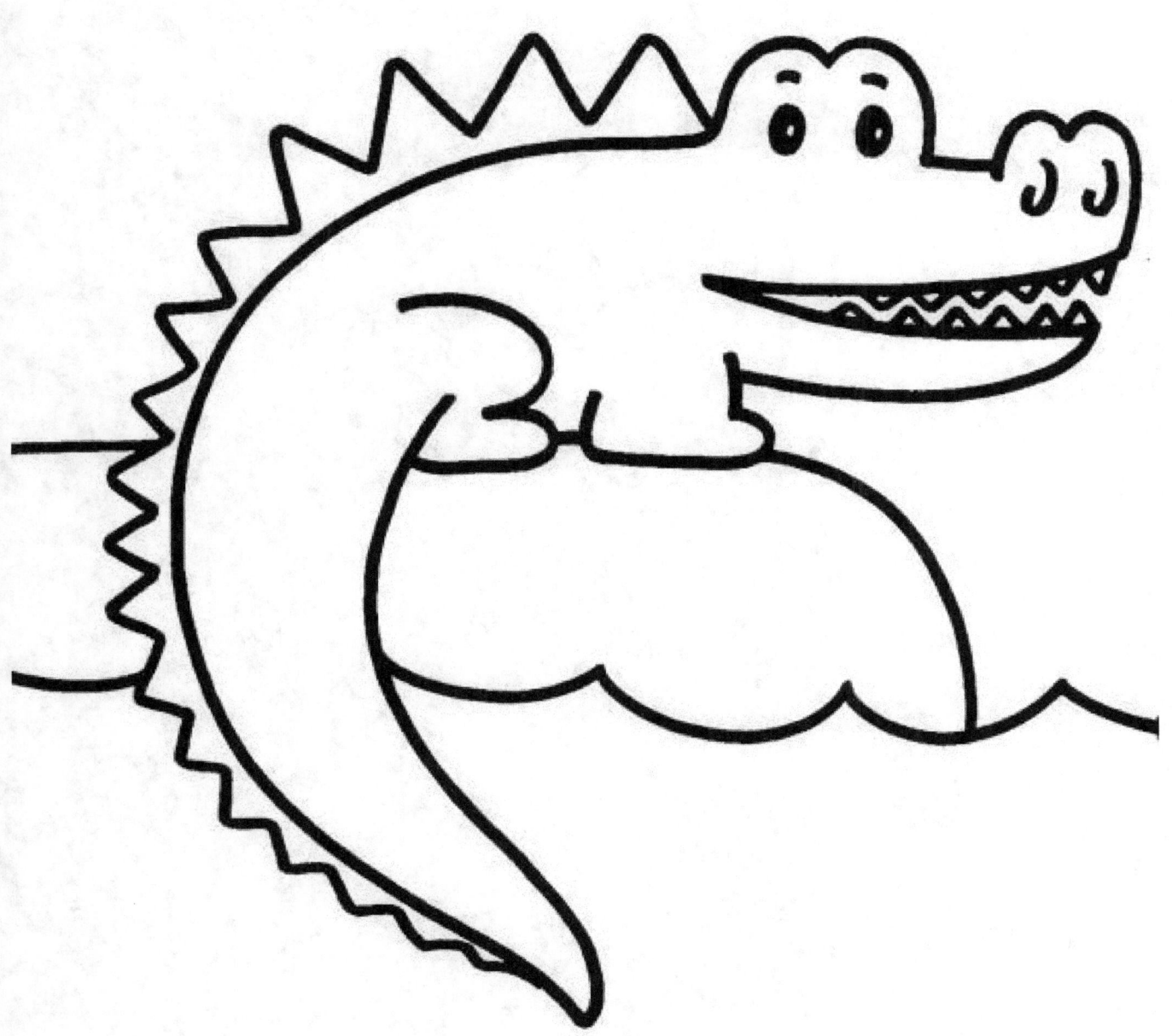

Kangaroo - Canguro

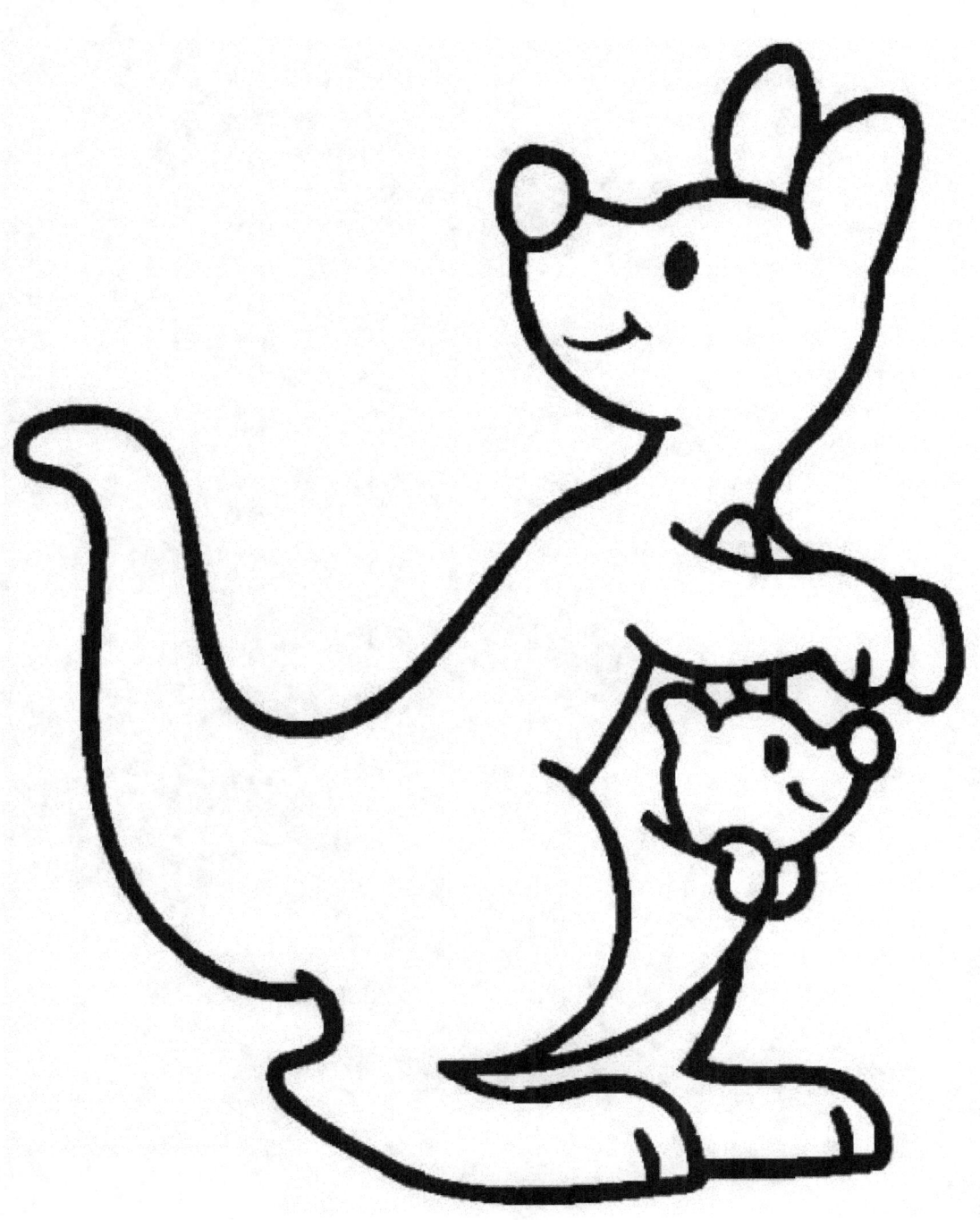

Lion - León

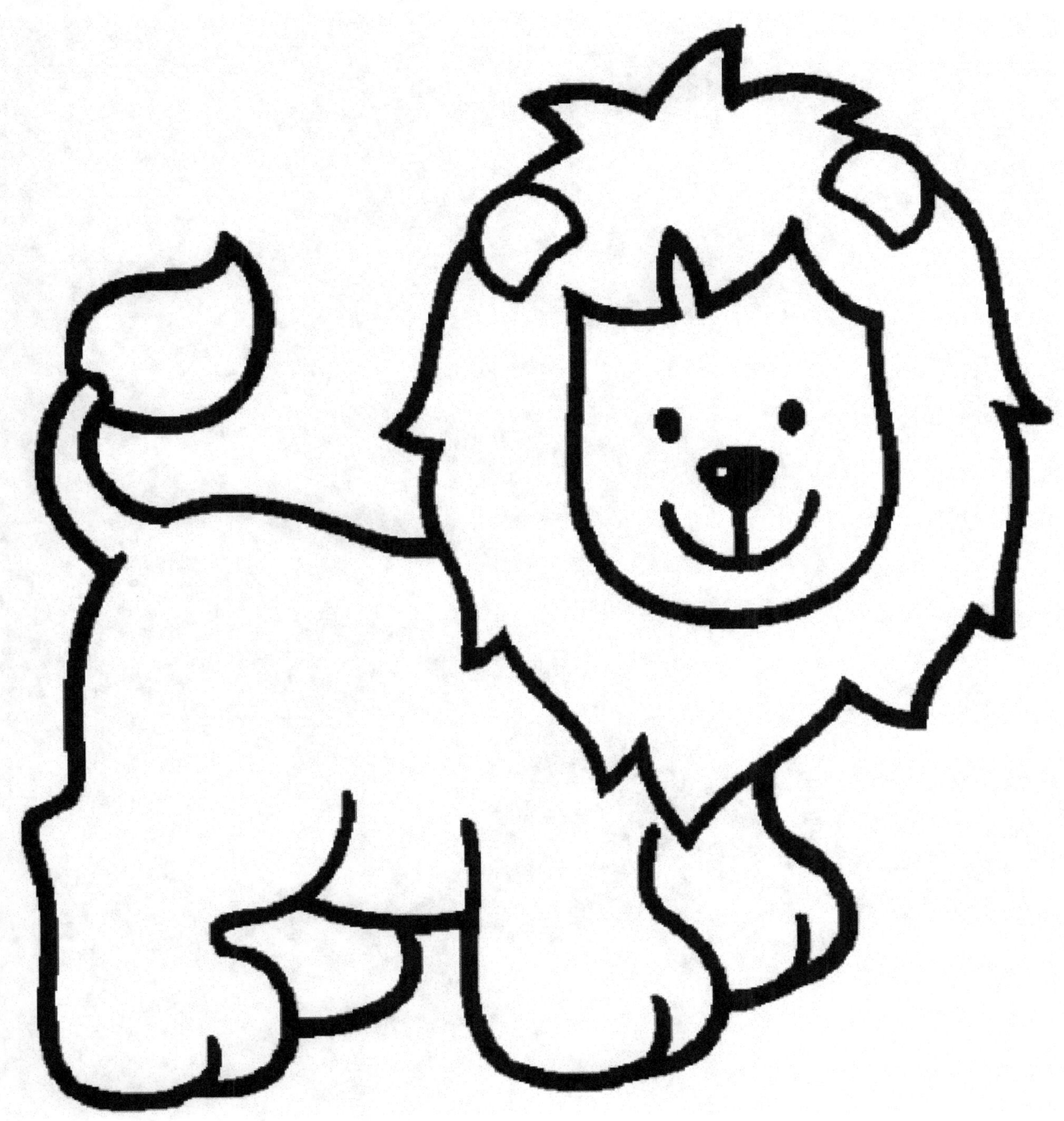

Giraffe - Jirafa

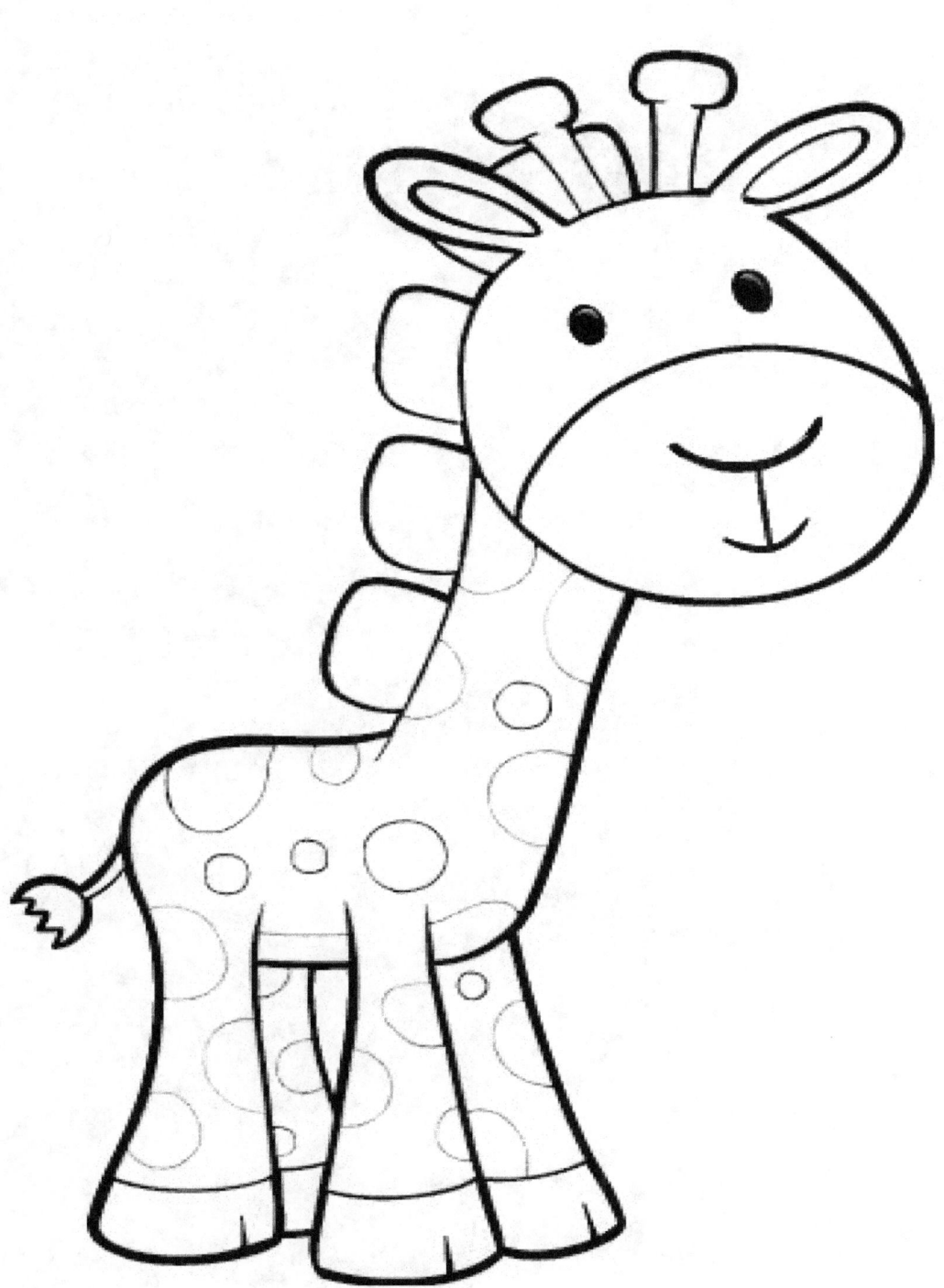

Monkey - Mono

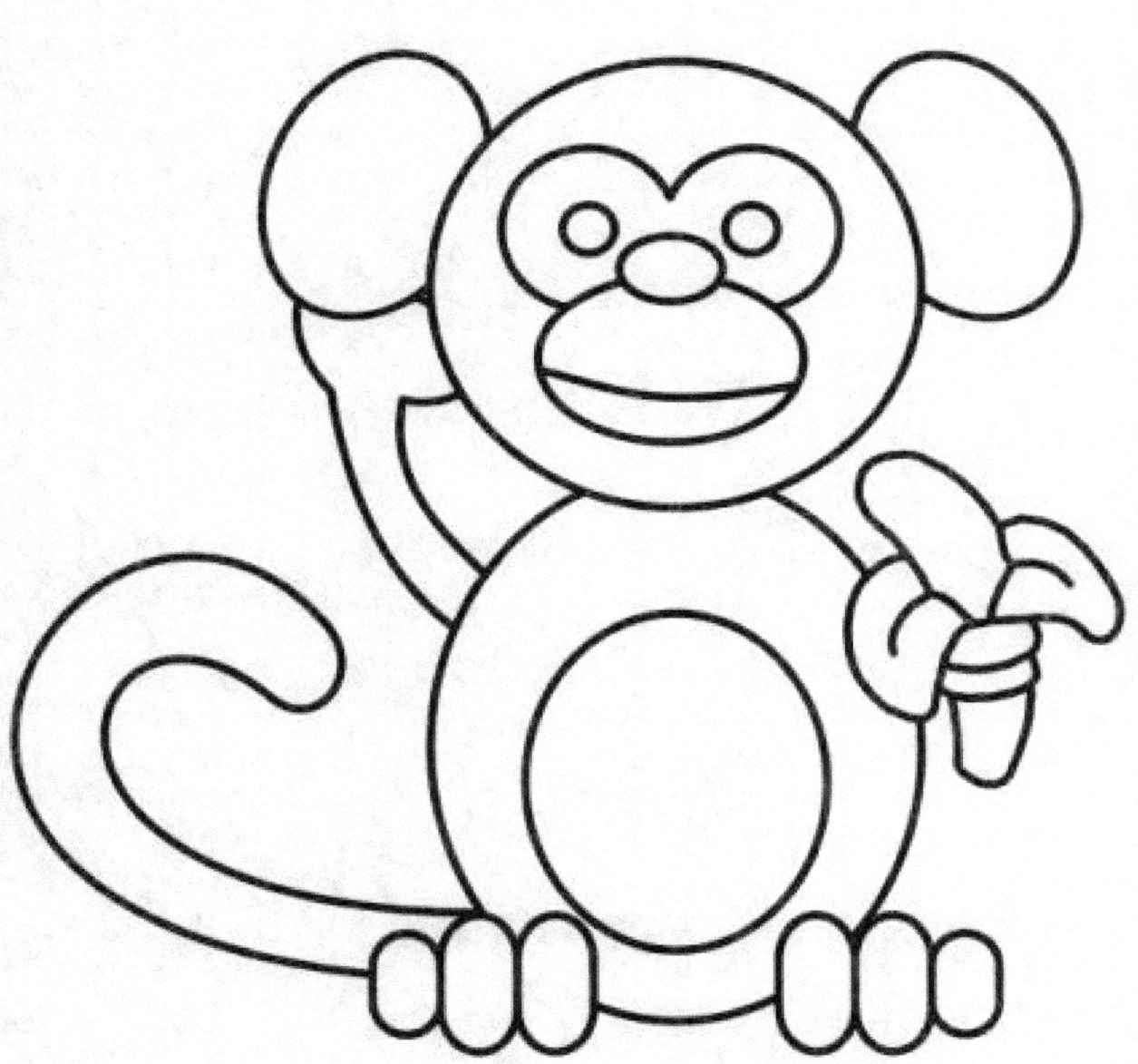

Elephant - Elefante

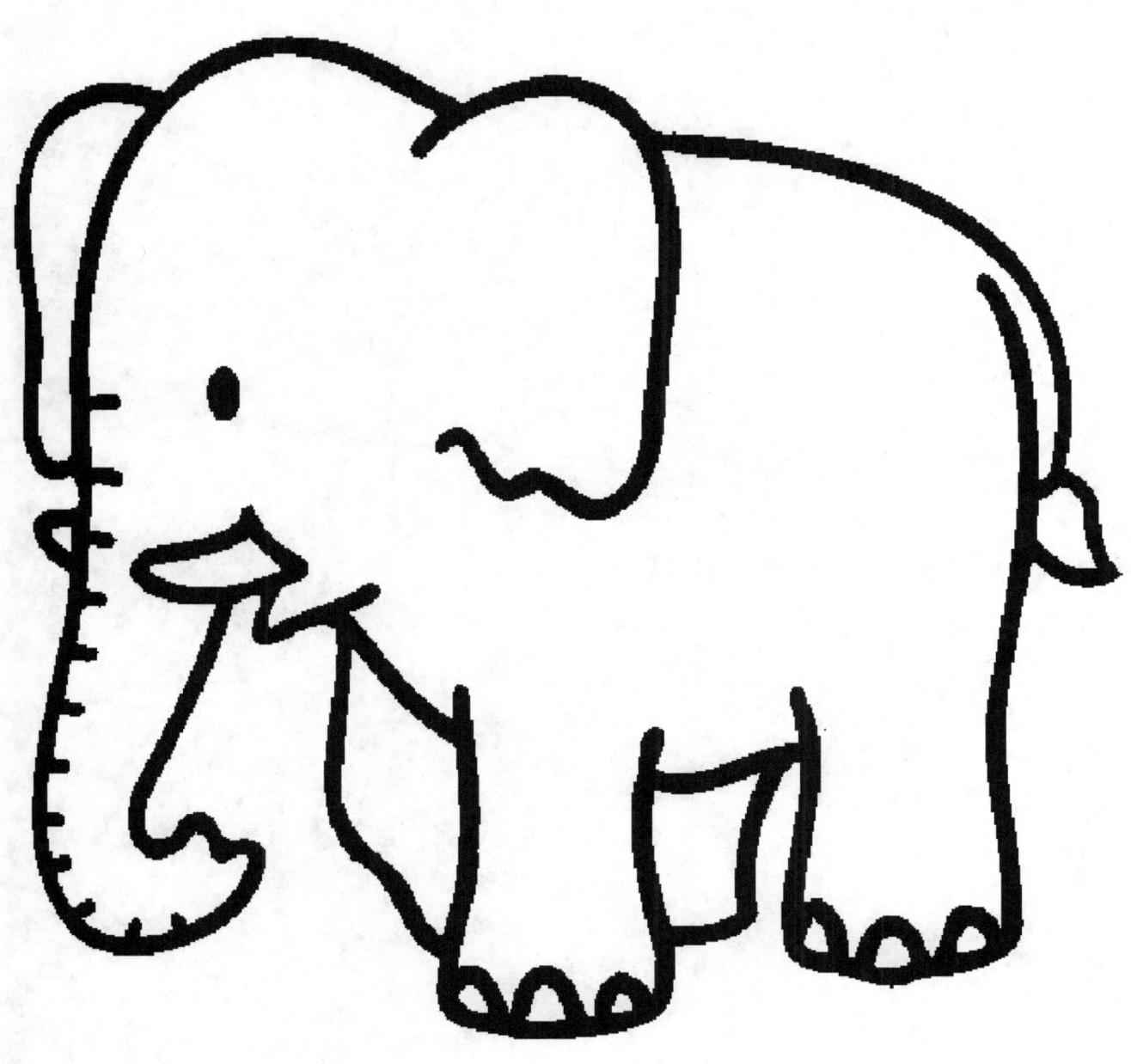

Bear - Oso

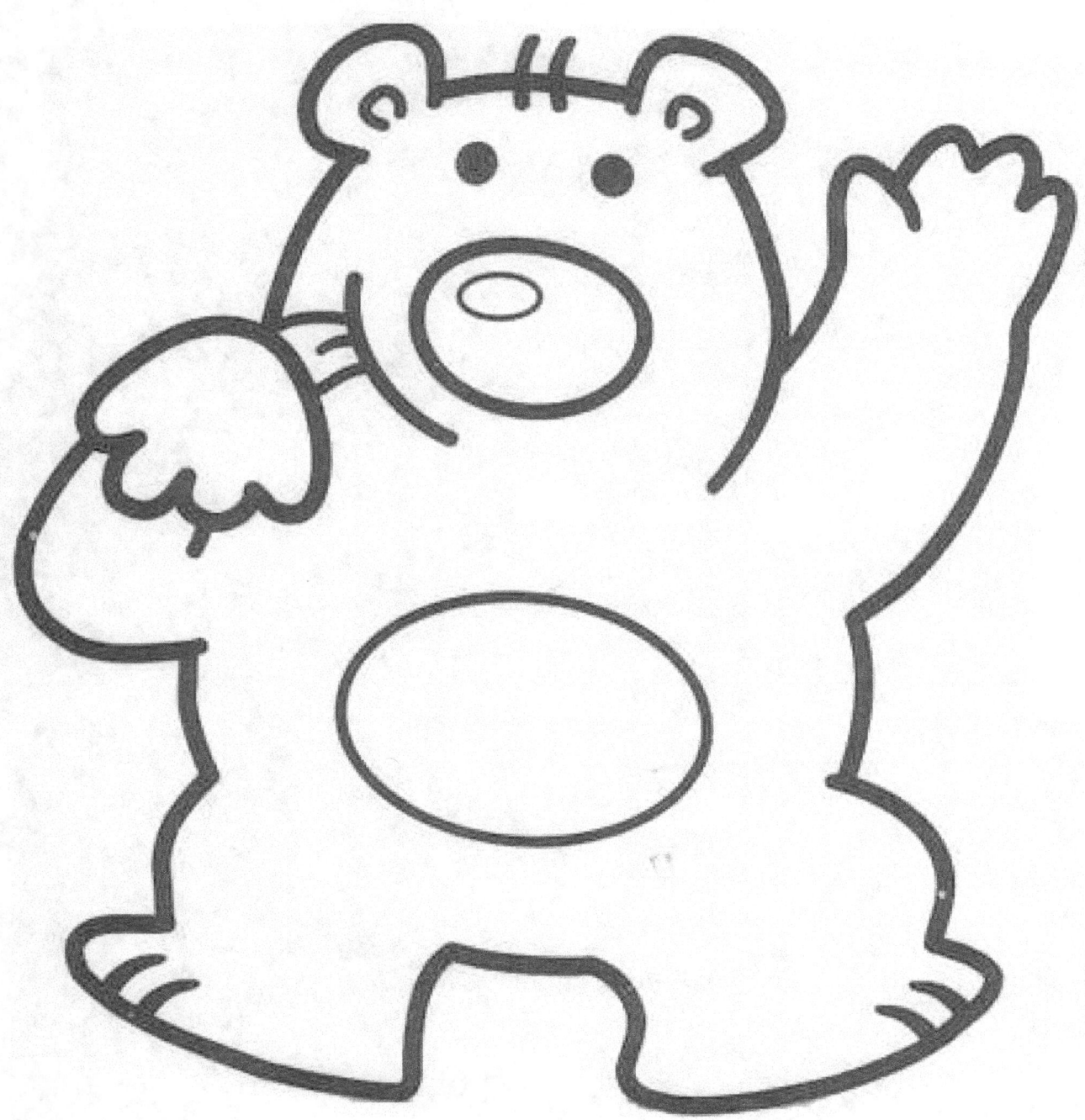

Dinosaur - Dinosaurio

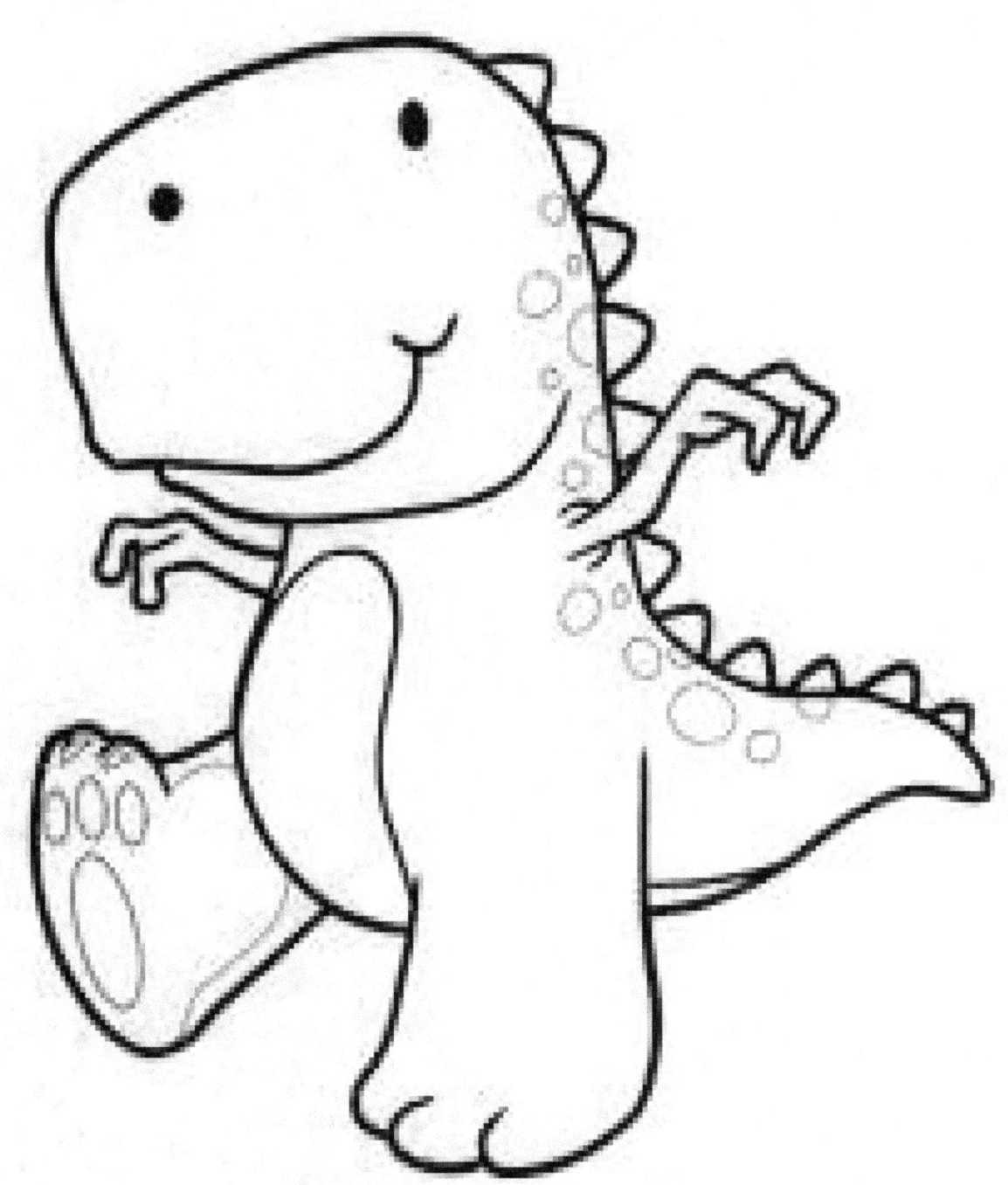

Unicorn - Unicornio

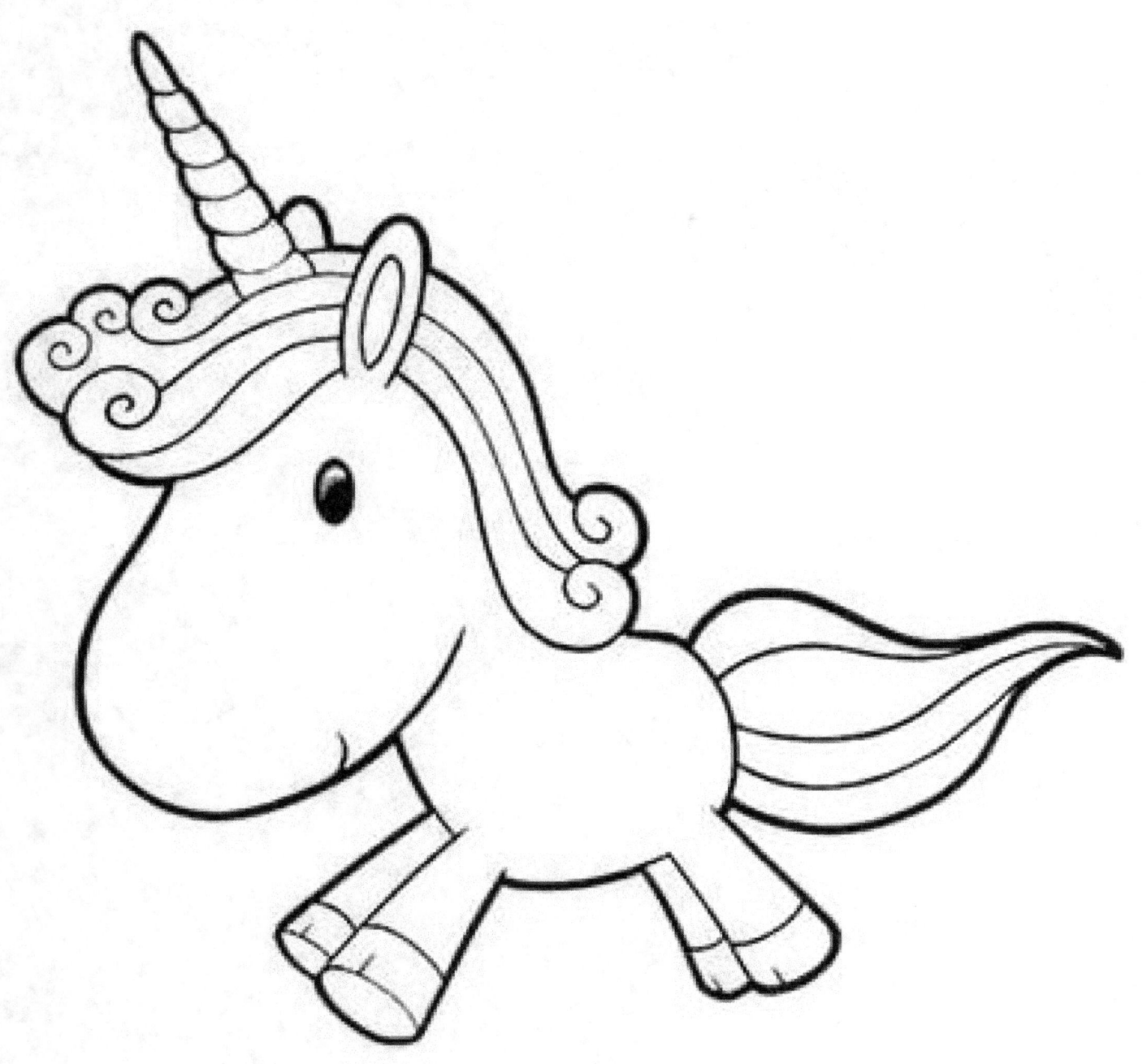

www.ingramcontent.com/pod-product-compliance
Lightning Source LLC
Chambersburg PA
CBHW060434220526
45465CB00008B/3138